New English One-act Plays

James Saunders · David Campton
Lyndon Brook · Roy Minton

Model Interpretations

By Peter Pasch

Ernst Klett Verlag

Acknowledgements

James Saunders, *Over the Wall* (1977) published in *Play Ten* ed. Robin Rook, is reprinted by permission of Edward Arnold, London.
For performing rights please contact the author's agent: Margaret Ramsay Ltd., 14a Goodwin's Court, St. Martin's Lane, London WC2N 4LL.

David Campton, *Incident* is reprinted by permission of J. Garnet Miller Ltd., Malvern, Worcestershire.
For amateur performing rights please contact J. Garnet Miller Ltd., 13 Tottenham Street, London W1. For professional rights applications should be made to Actat (Theatrical & Cinematic) Ltd., 16 Cadogan Lane, London SW1.

Lyndon Brook, *Score*, published in *Double Act* ed. Mark Shackleton is reprinted by permission of Edward Arnold, London.
For performing rights please contact the author's agent: Margaret Ramsay Ltd., 14a Goodwin's Court, St. Martin's Lane, London WC2N 4LL.

Roy Minton, *Bovver* is reprinted by permission of Marjacq Scripts Ltd., London.
For performing rights please contact the author's agent: Marjacq Scripts Ltd., 32 Cumberland Mansions, Nutford Place, London W1H 5ZB.

The texts to which these interpretations refer are also available in a student's edition: New English One-act Plays (Klettbuch 57825).

A recorded version of the one-act plays interpreted here is available on cassette (Klettnummer 57827).

1. Auflage 1 6 5 4 3 2 | 2002 2001 2000 99 98

Alle Drucke dieser Auflage können im Unterricht nebeneinander benutzt werden, sie sind untereinander unverändert. Die letzte Zahl bezeichnet das Jahr dieses Druckes.

Umschlaggestaltung: Hans Lämmle, Stuttgart.
Druck: Gutmann + Co GmbH, 74388 Talheim. Printed in Germany.
ISBN 3-12-578260-0

Inhalt

Preface to the Student's Book

The short plays in this collection were written by four contemporary British playwrights and deal with some of the problems of modern British society. They have been chosen for their psychological interest as well as for the possibilities of performance they offer in the classroom or on the stage.

There are some short biographical notes on the authors at the end of each play.

The annotations at the bottom of each page are divided into two categories: the words and expressions which should be learned for active use are in bold type; those that are explained merely to facilitate comprehension are in normal type. The numbers refer to the lines.

Abbreviations:

coll.	colloquial	*s.o.*	someone
sl.	slang	*s.th.*	something
lit.	literary		

Einführung

Die vorliegende Ausgabe enthält eine Sammlung von *One-Act Plays*[1], die verschiedene Probleme der heutigen Zeit literarisch thematisieren. *Over the Wall* ist eine humorvolle *fable of our time, Bovver* stellt subtil-raffiniert die Relativität von Recht und Gerechtigkeit zur Diskussion, *Incident* befaßt sich mit dem Thema des Außenseiters, und *Score* arbeitet das Problem des erbarmungslosen Konkurrenzkampfes psychologisch vielschichtig auf[2]. Alle erst in jüngster Zeit entstandenen Dramen sind *well-made plays*, die sich insofern gut als Bausteine für den Unterricht eignen, als sie – im Gegensatz zu einem abendfüllenden Werk – einen schnellen und zielgerichteten Zugriff auf die jeweiligen Themen ermöglichen. Sie bieten in sprachlich und strukturell verständlicher Form die Möglichkeit, größere landes- bzw. kulturkundliche Unterrichtsreihen fiktional zu ergänzen und zu bereichern, wobei sie die betreffenden Themen künstlerisch verfremdet und humorvoll, ironisch, satirisch, provokativ oder in „absurden Situationen" aufgreifen und präsentieren. Selbstverständlich können die hier ausgewählten Kurzdramen auch als „literarische Inseln" zur Erweiterung der literarischen und kulturellen Kompetenz der Schüler beitragen.

Alle Kurzdramen konfrontieren die Schüler mit Konflikten, Problemen, Vorstellungen und Ansichten, die zu Gesprächen und Auseinandersetzungen führen und zu Wertentscheidungen veranlassen können. Spannung, Mehrdeutigkeit und Offenheit als besondere Merkmale des *short play* als literarische Textsorte ermöglichen immer wieder Empathie und Identifikation.

Darüber hinaus ergeben sich auch Sprechanlässe aufgrund der Gattungsspezifik des literarischen Genres, d. h. aus der sprachlichen, thematischen, handlungsmäßigen und bühnentechnischen Konzentration und Reduktion auf das Wesentliche. Die strikte Einheit von Ort und Zeit bewirkt eine Einheit der Atmosphäre, die genauso zu Gesprächen und Diskussionen Anlaß geben kann wie der Verzicht auf optisch-realistische Verständnishilfen oder auf breit angelegte Anfangsexpositionen. Der signifikante Augenblick, die Krisen- oder Endsituation steht im Mittelpunkt: Die reduzierte Zahl der *characters*, die intensive Sprache, der Schwund an epischer Substanz tragen dazu bei, daß der Leser/Schüler/Zuschauer stets mitarbeiten, ergänzen oder sogar – wie bei *Score* – den Ko-Text geradezu rekonstruieren

1 Der Begriff '*One-Act Play*' wird in der fachdidaktischen Diskussion meist ersetzt durch den Terminus '*Short Play*'.

2 In den jeweiligen Vorbemerkungen zu den Interpretationen werden die thematischen Bereiche differenziert aufgeführt.

muß. Auch der z. T. offene Schluß der Dramen ist hervorzuheben, weil das Fehlen einer Lösung die Schüler herausfordert[3].

Im Gegensatz zu anderen literarischen Gattungen sind die Kurzdramen nicht nur als Wort- sondern auch als Bühnenkunstwerke und damit als synästhetische Texte anzusehen. An ihnen lassen sich nicht nur Bauformen wie *plot, character* oder *structure* analysieren, sie eröffnen auch eine neue kreative Dimension: Durch das Lesen mit verteilten Rollen, durch eigene Ton- und Videoaufnahmen und nicht zuletzt durch eigene Theateraufführungen können die Kurzdramen auf der Ebene der Regie die Phantasie, den Erfindungsgeist und die Experimentierfreude anregen und damit die Motivation steigern[4]. Die Schüler können im schöpferischen Spiel positive Erfahrungen sprachlicher und gestalterischer Art machen.

Die Frage, ob man die Dramen genau lesen und literarisch umfassend interpretieren und analysieren soll (*close reading*), oder ob man sie lediglich „genießen" sollte (*reading for fun*), muß von Fall zu Fall beantwortet werden. Es ist verständlich, daß sich der Lehrer/die Lehrerin ständig im Dilemma zwischen „prodesse und delectare" befindet, zwischen einer kritisch fundierten und intensiven Analyse einerseits und der Zielvorstellung andererseits, den Schülern durch Gewährung eines Freiraums und unter Verzicht auf wissenschaftspropädeutischen Ehrgeiz den Weg zu öffnen, Lektüre zu genießen, um sie als „lebenslange Privatleser" zu erhalten. Beide Wege müssen sich natürlich nicht unbedingt ausschließen.

Insofern sind die vorgeschlagenen Interpretationen eher als pragmatische Angebote und als praxis-orientierte Anleitung zu verstehen. Wortangaben, Fragestellungen, Tafelbilder, Diagramme, Arbeitsaufträge etc. sind aus dem Unterricht entstanden und als Vorschläge zur Arbeitserleichterung für die kreative Gestaltung des eigenen Unterrichts zu betrachten.

Das *Glossary of Literary Terms* am Ende dieses Lehrerbuches umfaßt Begriffe, die bei der Interpretation oder Inszenierung der Kurzdramen benötigt werden könnten. Es kann den Schülern – je nach Bedarf – ganz oder in Auszügen ausgehändigt werden.

---

[3] Eine gute, auch für Schüler verständliche Darstellung der literarischen Charakteristika des short play befindet sich bei Albert-Reiner Glaap, *Alan Ayckbourn: Confusions – Model Interpretations*, (Klett-Nr. 57953), Seite 6–7.

[4] Die angebotene Cassettenaufnahme kann in dieser Hinsicht als eine von vielen möglichen „Interpretationen" des Texts betrachtet werden.

James Saunders

Over the Wall

Characters:
Narrator (N)
Other speakers (numbered 1–9)

N: There was once an island, if you believe it, on which lived a people no better and no worse than most. They had enough to eat, without stuffing themselves, everyone had a day's work (which in those times was considered a great blessing), the old were looked after, as long as they didn't outstay their welcome, and the young were respected as individuals – within reason. All this had been so for as long as anyone could remember, and so they hoped it would continue. For, while they were not exactly happy, they were not exactly unhappy either. And as they said to each other when they bothered to talk about it:

1: If it was good enough for my father it's good enough for me. That's what my father used to say, and it's what I say too.

2: Absolutely. Leave well alone, that's my motto.

3: We should count our blessings. It's better than it was in the bad old days.

4: Mind you, it's not so good as it was in the good old days.

5: But things could always be worse. That's what we should think of.

6: They could always be better, of course.

5: But they could always be worse.

7: At least we're allowed to work all day.

8: And we're allowed not to work on Saturday and Sunday.

9: And we've got the vote. We didn't have that in the bad old days.

6: (*female*) We didn't have it in the good old days.

N: So they counted their blessings and rested content. Now what made this island different from any other you might have in mind was a wall,

7	to stuff oneself	to eat more than necessary
8	**a blessing**	a gift from God, a good thing
9	to outstay one's welcome	to stay too long (as a guest)
16	to leave well alone	to make no change to something that is good
17	to count one's blessings	to remember how lucky one is
19	mind you	however

which ran across the island a bit more than halfway down and which had been there as long as anyone could remember, and as long as anyone they could remember could remember. For ever, in fact, as far as they knew or cared. They called it 'The Wall', and if they ever talked about it they said things like:

1: There's always been a Wall and there always will be, that's the way things are. It's a fact of nature. There's nothing you can do about it.

2: There must be a purpose in it, that's what I say. Everything has its purpose: wars, walls, it's all meant.

3: There are things beyond us. A higher Wall, I mean Will. Someone's in charge up there. The great Wall-Builder in the sky. He knows what's best for us. Leave it to Him, that's what I say.

6: Or Her.

4: After all, when you think of us – human beings – crawling on the earth . . . I mean humility's called for. It's not for us to seek to understand the sublime purpose.

5: *Of* which the Wall is part.

4: *Of* which the Wall is part.

1: It was good enough for my father, and it's good enough for me. That's what my father used to say. Leave it at that. Nuff said.

N: So they went on with their business, working as they were allowed to through the week, and on Saturdays and Sundays working, as they were allowed to, at what they called their leisure activities. This wall, now, was not quite straight but curved outwards, so that you could never see the two ends of it together. Not that it had ends for, as the fishermen knew, it continued, when it reached the sea, back along both shores to meet itself again at the far end of the island, so encircling the half of it – a bit more than half.

7: Lor, Jarge, yon Wall goos roit raind the oisland.

9	**meant** [ment] (past participle of *mean*)	intended
10	**beyond**	outside the range or limit of
	to be in charge	to be responsible
15	**humility** [hjuːˈmɪlətɪ]	modesty, humbleness
	called for	needed, necessary
16	**sublime** [səˈblaɪm]	causing deep feelings of wonder and admiration
20	Nuff said. *(coll.)*	Enough has been said.
23	**leisure** [ˈleʒə]	free time
29	Lor, Jarge, yon Wall goos roit raind the oisland.	Lord, George, that wall goes right round the island. (Imitation of the dialect spoken in country areas of the south-west of England)

8: Oi knoos thaat, Taam. Tis a well-knoon faact.

N: So they spoke when they fished. High it was, and smooth, and impregnable, and how it got there no one knew. There were theories, of course.

9: There is no doubt that it was constructed in the Neoplasticene Age by primitive tree-worshippers, to enclose the sacred grove of the earth-goddess ...

1: It was built of course, by invading Venusians, as a navigational aid and to protect the space-ships from marauding dinosaurs.

2: Obviously a natural outcrop of rock, pushed up by volcanic activity and then worn smooth by the wind and rain, an interesting phenomenomenom.

3: It's a figment of the imagination. The Wall only exists in our minds. If we stopped thinking it was there, it wouldn't be.

N: No one could prove this theory wrong.

4: I walked into it last night in the dark. Look at the bump on my forehead.

3: Psychosomatic. You *imagined* it was there, so when you got to where you imagined it was, you walked into it and imagined you hurt yourself. It stands to reason.

4: It still hurts.

3: You think it does.

N: But since it seemed to make not much difference, if you thought you walked into it, whether you were really hurt or only thought you were, people tried not to. Except for one poor fellow who so convinced

1	Oi knoos thaat, Taam. Tis a well-knoon faact.	I know that, Tom. It's a well-known fact.
2	impregnable [ɪm'pregnəbl]	which cannot be taken by force or penetrated
5	Neo-plasticene [ˌni:əʊ'plæstɪsi:n]	invented word reminding the reader of *Pleistocene* ['plaɪstəʊsi:n] (a geological era in the distant past) and *Plasticine* (trade mark of a soft claylike substance used for modelling)
6	a grove [əʊ]	a group of trees, a small wood
9	marauding [mə'rɔ:dɪŋ]	wandering about plundering and causing damage
10	an outcrop (of rock) ['– –]	a large rock or group of rocks sticking out of the ground
11	phenomenomenom	The speaker means *phenomenon.* [fɪ'nɒmɪnən]
13	a figment ['– –]	something that is not real but only imagined
16	a bump	a raised, round swelling
20	its stands to reason	it is clear to all sensible people, it is obvious

himself that the wall was imaginary that he took a flying leap at where it was, or wasn't, and dashed his brains out. Or so it seemed.

5: Excuse me, I'm conducting a survey. May I ask what *you* think is on the other side of the Wall?

6: I don't want to talk about it. I think it's disgusting. There's enough nasty *this* side of the Wall, never mind the *other* side of the Wall.

7: It's like a beautiful garden, with fruit hanging down and bambis and pretty flowers. And you don't have to wear any clothes.

8: It's like a sort of a ooze, a sort of – like a – ooze, sort of.

9: Nothing.

5: Nothing?

9: Nothing. Everything finishes at the Wall. Then there's nothing.

1: The fifth dimension.

2: Ethereal vibrations.

3: That is to say, beyond the Wall the laws of space-time as we know them no longer operate. Call it ethereal vibrations, call it the fifth dimension, call it a rolypoly pudding …

1: In other words, as far as we're concerned it doesn't exist in there – if one can say 'in there' for a 'there' which doesn't exist and therefore cannot be said to be either *in* or *there*. As for *what* doesn't exist …

3: It's like a mathematical point really …

9: Like I said, nothing.

2: Don't know.

3: Don't know.

4: Don't know.

6: Don't care.

N: So there it was. Or wasn't, or was in a different way, or seemed to be.

1: Mum!

2: What?

1: What's over the Wall?

1	to take a flying leap	to take one big jump
2	He dashed his brains out.	He killed himself by hitting his head against the wall.
3	**a survey** ['sɜ:veɪ]	*here:* a study of opinions *(Meinungsumfrage)*
7	a bambi	a baby deer (cf. Walt Disney's film 'Bambi')
9	ooze [u:z]	mud; thick, sticky liquid
14	ethereal [ɪ'θɪərɪəl]	of unearthly lightness and delicacy
17	a rolypoly pudding [ˌrəʊlɪ'pəʊlɪ]	a pudding made of pastry spread with jam or fruit which is rolled and baked or steamed

2: You wash your mouth out with soapy water! I'll give you over the Wall! Wait till I tell your father!

3: Dad!

4: What?

3: What's over the Wall?

4: Ask your teacher. What d'you think I pay rates and taxes for? To teach you myself?

3: I asked my teacher.

4: Well?

3: Said to get on with my algebra.

4: Well, then, do what your teacher says.

3: But what *is* over the Wall?

4: The toe of my boot. Get on with your homework.

3: I've done my homework. What *is* over the –?

4: Then do something else. Can't you see I'm trying to watch telly?!

N: Or whatever it was they watched in those days; it wasn't telly.

4: Can't you see I'm trying to watch the goldfish?

5: Can't you see I'm trying to get this ferret out of my trousers?

6: Can't you see I'm trying to invent the wheel?

7: – cook the joint?

8: – bath the baby?

9: – darn my socks?

4: – frame a photo of my mother?

5: – write a sonnet?

6: – make a fortune?

7: – get my head out from between these railings?

8: – bury the cat?

9: – dig a well starting at the bottom?

N: Or whatever. And so, in short, on the whole, more or less, without splitting hairs, broadly speaking, in a nutshell, they ignored it.

1	You wash your mouth out with soapy water!	Stop using bad language! (said to children)
	I'll give you …	Don't give me that nonsense about …
18	a ferret	*Frettchen*
	I'm trying to get this ferret out of my trousers.	A traditional sport in some country districts of England is to see how long you can keep a ferret inside your trousers.
20	a joint	a large piece of meat for roasting
22	to darn	to repair (stockings etc.) *(stopfen)*
30	**to split hairs**	to pay too much attention to unimportant differences
	in a nutshell	in brief; in as few words as possible

1: Pretended it wasn't there.

N: Well, no, they couldn't do that. Because it was. No, they just ... ignored it; as you might ignore a gatecrasher at a party whom nobody knows and nobody wants to, who turns up in the wrong gear with a nasty look on his face and what looks like a flick-knife sticking out of one pocket.

3: It's ridiculous.

2: What is?

3: It's stupid. I can't believe it. It's ludicrous. Here we are with a great Wall across the island and we don't even know why and no one seems to care.

2: It's not for us mere mortals to ask why.

3: Why not?

2: Because we're mere mortals, that's why not.

3: I'm not a mere mortal, I'm a rational human being.

5: We're not meant to understand everything, you know.

3: Why not, who says so?

6: There's enough needs putting right *this* side of the Wall, never mind the *other* side of the Wall.

7: Get on with your work and think yourself lucky. Thinking about the Wall won't do you any good.

8: Do some leisure activities, take your mind off it. Do some healthy outdoor pursuits.

4: All you do is talk about the Wall. Wall, Wall, Wall, that's all I get from you.

2: Leave wall alone, I mean leave well alone, that's my advice.

1: Ignorance was good enough for your father and it ought to be good enough for you.

4: Who do you think you are anyway? God or somebody?

3: I want to know what's on the other side!!

5: Next please. Well, now, what seems to be the matter with you?

3	a gate-crasher	s.o. who goes to a party without having been invited
4	gear [gɪə]	*here:* clothing for a particular purpose
5	a flick-knife	a knife with a blade that springs into position when a button is pressed
9	ludicrous ['lu:dɪkrəs]	ridiculous, absurd
12	**a mortal**	s.o. who is bound to die some day (i.e. a human being as opposed to a god)
18	There's enough needs putting right ...	There's enough that needs to be put right ...
23	outdoor pursuits	activities carried out in the open air

3: I'm having a bit of trouble, doctor.

5: What sort of trouble? Stick out your tongue.

3: It'th athout the Thall …

5: Put your tongue in.

3: It's about the Wall. All I want to know …

5: Bowel movements all right?

3: Yes, thanks. All I want to know is what's on the other side, that seems reasonable enough to me, only –

5: Sleeping all right, are you? Getting the old beauty sleep?

3: I dream about walls. Only no one else seems to be bothered, only me, so I –

5: How's your sex-life? Sex-life all right, is it? The old nudge nudge wink wink?

3: I'm not bothered, thanks. So I wondered if there's something wrong with me, or if in fact –

5: Eating all right, are you? Getting the old nosh down?

3: Yes, I'm eating. Or if in fact it's that there's something wrong with everybody else. And it's turning into a bit of –

5: How's the pains in the leg? Pains in the leg all right?

3: They're fine. Into a bit of an obsession. Because, I mean, you don't just ignore something like that, I mean I'm not a mere mortal, I'm a rational human being and it could be important, I mean, *look* at the flaming thing, I mean *look* at it, there it is, look, there!

5: Any neuralgia, headache, backache, loss of breath, vomiting, congenital idiocy, piles, trouble with the waterworks, spots before the eyes, dizzy spells?

6	**bowel movements** ['baʊəl]	the movements of the bowels *(Darmtätigkeit, Stuhlgang)*
12	to nudge s.o.	to push s.o. gently with the elbow
	to wink	to close one eye briefly, especially as a private signal
	nudge nudge wink wink	used when men talk humorously about sex
16	nosh *(sl.)*	food
20	**an obsession**	a fixed, often unreasonable idea that occupies the mind
22	flaming *(sl.)*	a mild swear word used for emphasis
24	neuralgia [ˌnjʊə'rældʒə]	sharp nerve pain
	to vomit ['vɒmɪt]	to be sick; to throw up the contents of the stomach through the mouth
	congenital [kən'dʒenɪtl]	existing from one's birth
25	piles	haemorrhoids
26	a dizzy spell	an attack of dizziness *(Schwindel)*

3: D – I – Z – Z –

5: Falling hair, loss of weight, gain of weight, tenseness, got a drink problem have you, smoking too much, hallucinations, palpitations, eructations, on drugs are you, can you read the top line, overdoing it at work perhaps, worrying about the work, about the spouse, about where to go for your holiday, about the mortgage, about the value of the pound, about the political situation, about your old mother, about the kids, kids playing you up are they, not doing well at school, got a drink problem have they, smoking, on drugs are they, suffering from loss of weight, falling hair, got any worries have you?

3: Yes!

5: Have you seen a priest?

3: Yes. She didn't know either.

5: Didn't know what? They're not supposed to know, they're supposed to give comfort. Seen a psychiatrist, have you, consulted a shrink?

3: He said it was my mother.

5: Well there you are. Here's a prescription. Take some four times a day, and if there's any left over, rub it on your chest. Or your mother's chest. I don't care.

3: What's wrong with me, doctor?

5: You're a nut. Get out, you're wasting my time.

N: So out he got, this nut, taking his obsession with him, and the doctor turned thankfully to the next patient, a nice simple case who'd put his thumb out trying to plant beans in hard ground.

5: Put your thumb out, have you? How's your bowel movements? Sleeping all right?

3: I'm going to start an Association For Investigating The Wall In Order To See What's On The Other Side. The AFITWIOTSWOTOS. Catchy title. They'll flock to join. Then we'll get somewhere.

2	tenseness	state of nervousness *(Angespanntheit)*
3	palpitations [ˌ––ˈ––]	irregular beating of the heart
	eructations [ˌiːrʌkˈteɪʃnz]	the rising of gas from the stomach through the mouth; belch
5	spouse [spaʊz] *(formal)*	wife
6	**a mortgage** [ˈmɔːgɪdʒ]	money borrowed from a bank to buy a house *(Hypothek)*
8	to play s.o. up *(coll.)*	to cause s.o. problems, pain or difficulties
15	a shrink *(sl.)*	psychoanalyst, psychiatrist
21	a nut *(sl.)*	a madman, a crazy person
27	to investigate [–ˈ–––]	to find out detailed facts about s.th.; to examine
28	catchy	easy to remember
29	**to flock**	to come together in great numbers

N: But they didn't. And after a while he disbanded the association, with the full agreement of the members – himself. But he didn't give up.

3: All right. I'm on my own. So be it. But I'm going to find out what's on the other side of that Wall. If it kills me.

N: And for the next thirty or forty years he did nothing but think about the Wall. He read books, consulted sages, took measurements, drew diagrams, worked out theories, studied history, biology, theology, psychology, astrology, cogitated, meditated and did a bit of yoga on the side. He lost his friends of course.

6: Oh, don't invite *him*. He'll only talk about the Wall.

N: His marriage went for a Burton.

4: Wall, Wall, Wall, nothing but Wall! I'm sick of Wall! And I'm sick of you too! I'm going home to Father!

N: Slam. His kids turned delinquent.

7: What are you doing tonight?

8: Thought I'd cripple a few fuzz.

7: We did that last night.

N: Until finally, old, alone and penniless, he decided on the direct approach, and built his great invention: a sort of a catapult, quite novel in those times, which could hurl an object, or a person, up to an enormous height. He tried it on a rock, which disappeared into the blue, and then, one day, surrounded by curious bystanders, sat his own skinny, threadbare old body where the rock had been.

3: Wind it up, then.

N: They did.

3: When I say three, pull the lever. One ... two ... thr ... ooww!

N: They did, only too glad to get rid of this nut, this disruptive influence, so they could get back to watching their goldfish and planting their beans.

9: There he goes!

1	to disband an organization	to cause an organization to stop operating
6	a sage [seɪdʒ]	a very wise man
8	**to cogitate** ['kɒdʒɪteɪt]	to think deeply about s.th.
11	to go for a Burton *(sl.)*	to be destroyed, to be ruined
14	**delinquent** [dɪ'lɪŋkwənt]	committing minor crimes
16	fuzz *(sl.)* [fʌz]	policemen, the police
22	threadbare ['θredbeə]	thin, shabby, worn out
26	**a lever** ['li:və]	a bar used for lifting s.th. heavy
27	disruptive	causing disorder

1: Look at his rags flapping!
2: Bald head glinting in the sun!
4: Better than fireworks!
5: Coo!
N: Up he went, up, up, up, until looking down … we surmise … he saw the whole gold of that sunny day, the whole spread of the earth and seas, saw the tiny moving figures of people and the infinite distances of space. And it looked good.
3: I'm up! I'm over! I can see! I can see over! It's … It's … It's … Aaah!
N: A heart attack – we surmise. But in any case he was too far away for those on the ground to hear him. And as he dwindled into what seemed like a mathematical point, and disappeared, those on the ground shook their heads, or giggled, and went back to their beans, and their goldfish.

1	**rags**	old worn-out clothes
	to flap	to move quickly up and down or from side to side
2	**bald** [bɔːld]	without hair
	to glint	to sparkle, to shine brightly
4	Coo!	exclamation of surprise
5	to surmise *(formal)*	to suppose, to guess
11	to dwindle	to become steadily smaller
13	to giggle [ˈgɪgl]	to laugh in a silly or nervous way

Keystone, Hamburg

Biographical Notes

James Saunders was born in Islington in the East End of London in 1925. He was educated at Wembley County School and went on to read science at Southampton University. There he took up dramatic writing as a hobby, beginning with a few short plays. After finishing his studies he worked as a chemistry teacher. In 1963 the success of *Next Time I'll Sing to You* enabled him to devote himself to drama full time. The play tells the story of a hermit and reveals the utter loneliness of man as well as the impossibility of real communication. It was follwed by *A Scent of Flowers* (1964), a play which takes up similar problems.

Throughout his career, Saunders has written short, usually experimental plays in a variety of styles. Some of these plays are well known. *Alas, Poor Fred* investigates the problem of marriage, *A Slight Accident* (Klett: 'Modern One-act Plays') deals with the conflict between the desire to plan one's own life and the unpredictability of actual events.

Over the Wall was first published in a collection of short plays in 1977. Here a narrator tells the story of an island with a wall running across it. The Islanders' reaction to this apparently mysterious and unsurmountable obstacle is worked out in a number of episodes.

Unterrichtsvorschläge

Vorbemerkungen

1. Inhalt

Over the Wall ist ein lustiges und humorvolles Kurzdrama, in dessen Mittelpunkt ein Erzähler (N) steht. Er berichtet – ganz im Stil des *epic theatre* – von einer Insel und deren Bewohnern. Seine Erzählung wird jeweils unterbrochen und erweitert durch Beiträge von neun *voices*, die in kurzen dramatischen Szenen das facettenreiche Leben und die Lebenseinstellungen der Insulaner darstellen. Die Bewohner werden anfänglich als ganz zufrieden geschildert. Wenn sie sich überhaupt dazu bewegen lassen, etwas über sich und ihre Inselwelt zu erzählen, dann geschieht das meist dumpf über allgemeine Floskeln oder kleinkarierte Streitereien. Das Besondere an der Insel ist nun *the Wall*, eine Mauer, die sich quer über die Insel erstreckt und die absolute Grenze der Inselwelt darstellt. Woher diese Mauer kommt, welchen Sinn sie hat und was sich hinter ihr befindet, all diese Fragen bewegen die Inselbewohner eigentlich nicht so sehr. Eher schon erregt dieses Bauwerk das Interesse der Wissenschaften. Vor allem die Naturwissenschaften, die Theologie, die Philosophie, die Geologie, die Anthropologie und besonders die Psychologie haben genaue und wissenschaftlich abgesicherte Antworten auf die Frage, was es mit der Mauer auf sich hat. Es werden köstliche Hypothesen und vergnügliche Theorien aufgestellt, die der Erzähler mit trockenem Humor kommentiert und die von den Zuschauern (Schülern) mit Schmunzeln aufgenommen werden dürften, weil ergötzliche Parallelen zur heutigen Welt und Zeit möglich sind. Letztendlich jedoch bleibt die Mauer für die Inselbewohner irgendwie ein Rätsel, das weder durch öffentliche Umfragen, noch durch Kinderfragen gelöst werden kann. Lediglich ein einziger Inselbewohner (*the gatecrasher*) wagt sich ernsthaft an des Rätsels Lösung. Schließlich habe er als denkendes Wesen ein Recht auf die Beantwortung der Frage, was sich hinter dieser Mauer verbirgt. Aber plötzlich steht nun nicht mehr *the Wall*, sondern er selbst im Mittelpunkt des Interesses. Er wird wegen seiner *obsession* zum Ärgernis. Zunächst erhält er Ratschläge, dann Warnungen. Nachdem selbst Ärzte, Priester und Psychologen nichts mehr mit ihm anfangen können, wird er zum totalen Außenseiter, der sich endlich nach jahrelangen Forschungen selbst *over the Wall* in den Himmel katapultieren läßt, wo er schließlich die Wahrheit erfährt. Nur der Erzähler kann ihn begleiten. Die Insulaner sind froh, daß sie dieses *disruptive element* endlich los sind und daß sie sich wieder selbstzufrieden ihren Alltagsbeschäftigungen (*their beans and their goldfish*) zuwenden können.

In diesem Sinn kann *Over the Wall* als Parabel aufgefaßt werden, die die

Kleinkariertheit der Menschen, ihre Abhängigkeiten und Leitziele humorvoll und witzig aufs Korn nimmt.

2. Methodische Hinweise

Over the Wall ist sprachlich und inhaltlich leicht zu erfassen. Die klare Strukturierung des *short play* in deutlich abgegrenzte Erzähl- und Szenenabschnitte erleichtert den Zugriff auf das Werk. Es wäre daher für die praktische Unterrichtsarbeit sinnvoll, die einzelnen Episoden vor Beginn der Lektüre zu markieren bzw. zu numerieren.

Die vorliegenden Unterrichtsvorschläge ermöglichen ein variables und individuelles Vorgehen, das die Textarbeit durch Fragen, Arbeitsaufträge, Hausaufgaben, Diagramme, Skizzen und Tafelbilder abwechslungsreich absichert und Diskussionen anregt. Im Unterricht haben sich zwei Vorgehensweisen bewährt. Einmal kann eine intensive Lektüre erfolgen, die sich am vorliegenden Konzept orientiert. Zum anderen bietet sich auch eine kursorische Lektüre an. Sie entspricht einem *listening for gist and fun*, und zwar in dem Sinne, daß die Cassette gehört wird (bei geöffneten Büchern) und lediglich die *comic elements* zum Thema des Unterrichtsgesprächs gemacht werden.

Der Einsatz der Cassette ist sehr empfehlenswert, da die unterschiedlichen *voices* den Text stimmlich so interessant interpretieren, daß die Schüler erfahrungsgemäß viel Spaß daran haben.

3. Over the Wall als Theaterstück

Das Stück ist für 10 Sprecher (*narrator* + 9 *voices*) geschrieben, doch die Dialogparts können auch auf mehr – oder weniger – als 9 *voices* umverteilt werden.

Aufgrund dieser Vielzahl und Variabilität der Sprecher bietet sich in jeder Unterrichtsphase das **Lesen mit verteilten Rollen** an, da sehr viele Schüler aktiviert und motiviert werden können. Das gleiche gilt auch für eine **Cassetten-Aufnahme** durch die Schüler. Darüberhinaus empfiehlt sich ein ***playreading*** des Werks. Im Klassenzimmer kann schnell eine Spiel- und Aktionsfläche geschaffen werden, wobei z. B. die Spielerschar (*voices*) auf der einen Seite sitzen und der *narrator* auf der anderen Seite steht. Von dort aus kann er mit einem Zeigestock auf eine auf der Tafel aufgezeichnete Insel (+ *Wall*) zeigen und seine Erzählung beginnen. Die *playreaders* können dann zur Gestaltung des jeweiligen dramatischen Teils in die Mitte treten und ihrer Gestaltungsphantasie freien Lauf lassen. Auch auf der Bühne bedarf es weniger Mittel für die dramatische – und immer sehr motivierende – Darstellung. Es ergibt sich eine Fülle von Gestaltungsmöglichkeiten, die sogar Tonbildschauen mit Dias, Schatten- oder Handpuppenspiele einschließen können. Unterrichts- und Theatererfahrungen haben gezeigt, daß die Schülerkreativität gerade im Hinblick auf eine Bühnenrealisation sehr angeregt wird und zu dynamischen Vorbereitungsgesprächen im Unterricht führen kann.

Unit 1: The Island and the Wall (**3** 1–**8** 6)

Scene 1: **3** 1–**3** 27

Der Einstieg in das Kurzdrama erfolgt am besten über das Anhören der Cassette. Die Schüler werden sprachlich wohl wenig Verständnisschwierigkeiten haben und den Worten des deutlich und ruhig sprechenden *narrator* leicht folgen können. Durch die verschiedenen Stimmen mit den humorvollen Untertönen werden sie rasch in das Geschehen einbezogen.

1. *How does the narrator begin and what does he say about the setting of his 'story' (time and place)?*
The narrator begins his story like a fairy-tale: 'There once was an island . . .', thus placing it somewhere in a distant or imaginary past (cf. his ironical remark 'if you believe it') or rather in a state of timelessness. He doesn't mention the name of the island or any other geographical details, except that it is inhabited.

2. *What does the narrator tell us about the islanders?*
His description of the islanders is very vague and general, too. Although the word 'island' might evoke the notion of a wonderful utopia with all its promises of paradise, the narrator describes a people who have the same troubles and problems, share the same or similar feelings of happiness or unhappiness as any other people. Apparently the inhabitants of the island are living in a state of equilibrium, in which opposing opinions, forces and emotions are balanced – according to the narrator's humorous comments. The aspects of their life he chooses to point out are interesting in that food, labour and the care of the different generations are the essentials even of primitive life, and yet the audience are readily prepared to take up the challenge of drawing parallels with today's situation.

Notice the slight pause the narrator makes (on the cassette) before he makes his personal comment on these various aspects of their lives.

The islanders' situation can be portrayed on the board as follows. (The students can also work out the possible implications of the Narrator's comments):

This islanders	N.'s comment	Possible implications
– had enough food	... without stuffing themselves	→ a slight hint or 'dig' at people who eat too much
– had a day's work	... a great blessing in those days	→ it's a blessing in **our** days, too
– the old = looked after	... as long as they didn't outstay their welcome	→ eventually they were probably also sent to old people's homes, or otherwise 'disposed of'
– the young = individuals	... within reason	→ possibly the same restrictions were imposed on them as on today's young people
a 'happy' life	with restrictions	

3. *Describe the islanders' attitude towards their situation, as seen by the narrator.*
The islanders are satisfied with their situation and don't want it to change. They rarely take the time or the trouble to talk about it at all. It has been like this as long as they can remember, and they seem to be simply too lazy to imagine any alternatives.

4. *What is revealed when the islanders talk about their attitudes towards life?*
Whenever they bother to talk about it, some members of their society (voices 1 and 2) take refuge in clichés, which they apply as guides or as expressions of the aims and ideals of their lives. They would regard any change as a danger to their existence and convenience. They reveal a certain pig-headedness, inflexibility and insecurity.

Other islanders (voices 3–7) indulge in amusing comparisons between the past and the present. Some glorify the good old days. In return they are reminded that they should be humble and grateful as regards their present situation ('We should count our blessings'; **3** 17). The argument is again full of clichés and reveals a certain rigidity and dogmatism because each of the participants claims that his/her view is right without taking other opinions into account.

A third group of islanders (voices 7–9) reveals that they are in some way bound to a hidden authority that gives orders or permission (not) to do something ('we're allowed ...'; **3** 23/24)

In short, the people reveal a certain narrow-mindedness in that they argue fiercely about trifles and in that they are unable to escape the 'prison' of their clichés. They are, however, quite content.

Suggestions for the blackboard:

islanders' attitude towards life		people are reflected as
● – it was good enough for my father, it is good enough for me – leave well alone	tradition clichés	conservative inflexible insecure pig-headed
● – things are/could be – worse than – in good old days – better than – in bad old days	fuss about personal opinions	dogmatic petty argumentative
● we're allowed to – work all day – not on Sat/Sun – vote	dependence on some hidden authority	dependent
they reveal a certain 'pettiness'		BUT they are CONTENT ('dullness')

5. *What is the function of the narrator in the first scene?*
The narrator performs various functions:
- He tells a story (cf. Brecht's epic theatre) and is the 'creator' of the island and the people on it.
- He comments on what he creates; he comments on what people on the island do, how they react and how they feel (omniscient commentator).
- He establishes a connection with the audience by trying to involve them in his story ('if you believe it'; **3** 5). In addition, his humourous comments are definitely aimed at amusing the audience.
- He acts like a stage manager (cf. Thornton Wilder's *Our Town*) in that he gives a cue to the speakers to start speaking and ends their parts by making a brief summary of the main points (e.g. 'So they counted their blessing and rested content'; **3** 27).

Homework:
Give examples of humorous elements.
Much of the play's humour derives from the following elements:
- The narrator's humorous comments on the situation of the people in the introductory passage.
- The juxtaposition and amusing mixture of various clichés in the dramatic part (and the pleasant mixture of voices on the cassette).

– The enjoyable objection which is lodged by the female voice (voice 6).
– The narrator's final ironic remark ('So they counted their blessings and rested content'; **3** 27), which takes up one of the clichés uttered before (**3** 17).

Scene 2: **3** 27–**4** 23

In diesem Abschnitt wird *the Wall* eingeführt und die Stellungsnahme zu diesem Bauwerk seitens der Naturwissenschaften und der Theologie dramatisch persifliert.

Der Unterrichtsablauf sollte bei jeder *scene* aus Motivationsgründen methodisch variiert werden. An dieser Stelle würde es sich deshalb empfehlen, den zweiten Teil zunächst gemeinsam zu lesen (u. U. auch mit verteilten Rollen) und daran anschließend zu interpretieren. Dieses Vorgehen bietet sich auch deshalb an, weil der Text in den theologischen Passagen vom Druckbild her interessant ist (Großschreibung von *Wall, Will, Wall-Builder, Him, Her*). Abschließend kann dann die Cassette gehört werden, wobei besonders *voice 3* und *4* durch die leicht sakrale Stimmführung Heiterkeit auslösen dürften.

1. *How does the narrator introduce the Wall and what does he tell us about it?*
He points out that the Wall makes the island unique by addressing the audience personally ('... different from any other you might have in mind'; **3** 28). The Wall is a construction extending from one side of the island to the other, built long before anyone could remember. People have known it from time immemorial, but they don't worry about it; they hardly talk about it. The apparently precise description of its position ('a bit more than halfway down'; **4** 1) turns out to be humorously vague, and the time reference 'for ever' (**4** 3) pre-echoes the theological elements of the ensuing dramatic part.

Suggestions for the blackboard:

THE WALL

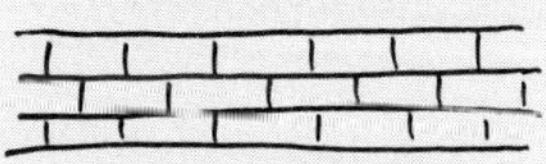

The N. addresses the audience

island = different from what you might have in mind

Where? Across the island. ← ... a bit more than halfway down

In existence since when? For ages. ← ... as long as anyone could remember
For ever (and ever)

People don't care.
They hardly talk about it.

humorous elements

2. *What do the islanders think of the Wall?*
Some (voice 1) regard the Wall as a 'fact of nature' (**4** 7), which will outlive everybody and last longer than anything else. And since man is bound to the limits of natural laws, he cannot do anything about it ('that's the way things are'; 'there's nothing you can do about it'). The Wall equals the 'wall' of natural laws which cannot be overcome or broken.

Other islanders (voices 2–6) refer to its possible origin and its possible function. They interpret it in terms of some vague purpose, and they begin to express and gradually enlarge on their own ideas, imaginings and phantasies about the meaning of the Wall's existence. They also draw conclusions and tell each other what the 'correct' attitude should be. What these voices say is amusing because it includes a lot of religious quotations and theological slogans and clichés.

Suggestions for the blackboard:

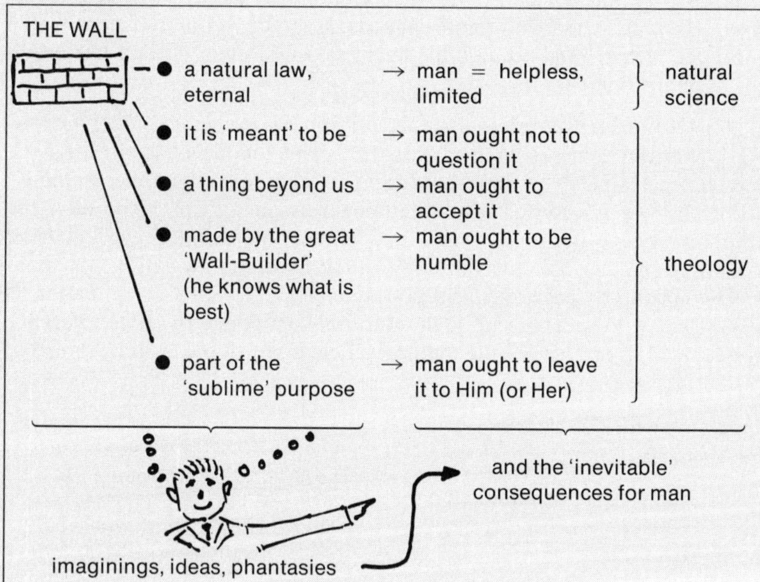

3. *What are the comic elements of this episode?*

Ironical elements:

- Voice 2 puts 'walls' and 'wars' on the same level, which conveys the meaning that even the deadly conflict or hostility among men has a 'purpose' and is not to be questioned (like the existence of the Wall).
- Voice 3 speaks of the great Wall-Builder (i. e. God) who, if understood in

the Christian sense, should be interested in breaking down barriers rather than creating them.

Humorous elements:

- the deliberate slip of the tongue: 'A higher Wall, I mean Will' (**4** 10)
- the reference to emancipation (or anti-sexist reference): 'Or Her' (**4** 13, voice 6 representing Women's Lib)
- theological elements which resemble a brief sermon:
  - everything has its purpose
  - it's all meant
  - there are things beyond us
  - a higher Will
  - someone's in charge up there
  - the great Wall-Builder in the sky
  - He knows what is best for us
  - leave it to Him
  - humility's called for
  - it's not for us to seek to understand the sublime purpose
- the use of capital letters: ***Wall-Builder, Him, Her, Will***
- the way in which the voices are juxtaposed. Nobody really listens to what the previous speaker says; everybody puts forward his/her ideas about the Wall ('that's what I say') with the help of explanations, interpretations, mock-analyses, clichés and sermon-like jargon. This constitutes blatant ridicule of theology.
- the way speaker 1 repeats his/her previous arguments (cf. **3** 14–15 and **4** 19) and the way he/she cuts the discussion short ('Leave it at that. Nuff said.').

Suggestions for summing up questions 2 and 3 on the board are made on p 26.

4. *How does the narrator conclude that scene?*

He concludes it similarly to the first one by humorously referring to the islanders' previously uttered belief that some hidden 'authority' allows them to work or not to work (cf. **3** 23–24).

Scene 3: 4 23–6 2

In diesem Teil kommt die Meinung anderer Wissenschaften auf humorvolle Weise zu Wort.

Es empfiehlt sich – wegen der Dialektpassagen –, die Bearbeitung dieses Teils mit dem Anhören der Cassette zu beginnen und auch abzuschließen. Dazwischen könnte das Unterrichtsgespräch durch folgende Fragen geleitet werden:

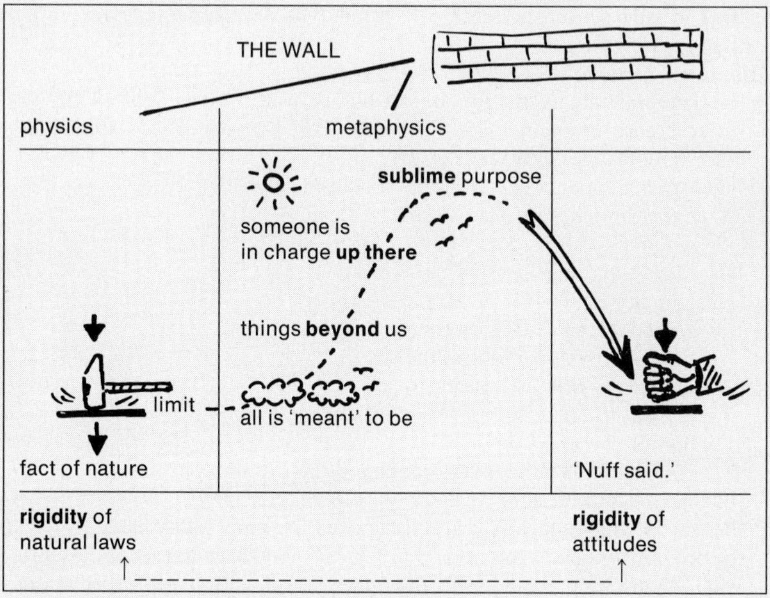

Blackboard suggestions for questions 2 and 3 on pp 24–25.

1. *What further elements is the Wall characterized by?*
The narrator enlarges the description of the *Wall* by referring to its shape: it is endless, surrounding more than half of the island (**4** 24–28). Furthermore it cannot possibly be surmounted, climbed, damaged or captured. It is strong and well-constructed (**5** 2–3).

In **5** 2–3 the narrator suddenly uses a kind of 'poetic' language (note the word order 'High it was ...' and the expressive adjectives), possibly as a humorous contrast to the ensuing scientific voices.

2. *What might be the function of the two fishermen's voices?*
What these simple people say and how they say it is meant to be a humorous and enjoyable contrast to the 'ethereal' language of the preceding voices as well as to the following 'scientific' notions.

3. *Describe the 'scientific' theories about the Wall.*
This dramatic part is definitely aimed at ridiculing the eagerness of scientists to use technical terms that sound extremely expert, but are in actual fact meaningless. The representatives of anthropology (voice 9), 'popular science' (here a sort of science fiction approach, voice 1), geology and psychology (voices 2 and 3) provide a very amusing mixture of nonsensical terms and yet emphasize that their theories are true. The truth and value of their notions, however, is only based on phrases like 'there's no doubt', 'of course', 'obviously', 'it stands to reason'.

Suggestions for the blackboard:

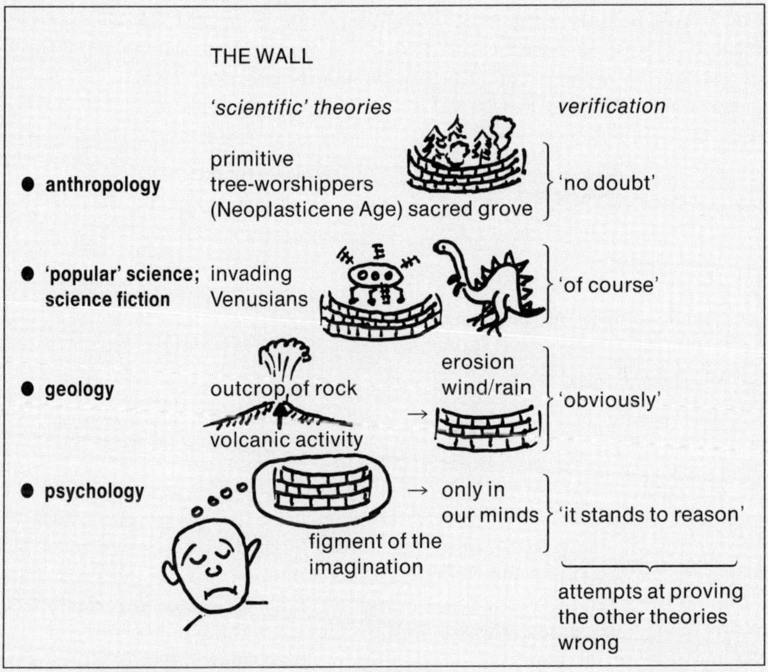

4. *How are the theories of science ridiculed?*
The satirical elements are:
- use of nonce-words: 'Neoplasticene Age', 'phenomenomenon'
- absurd sentences like 'If we stopped thinking it was there, it wouldn't be' (**5** 13–14) and the narrator's comment 'Nobody could prove this theory wrong' (**5** 15)
- juxtaposition of odd ideas and notions:
  'primitive tree-worshippers', 'the sacred grove of the earth-goddess', 'invading Venusians', 'a navigational aid', 'marauding dinosaurs', 'a natural outcrop', etc.
- the fact that the representatives of the different sciences insist on their theories although they can't prove them (cf. suggestions for the black board above).

Homework
How does the author develop the 'psychological' theory that the Wall only exists in people's minds?
The psychological theory is worked out to present a criticism of the

readiness (nowadays) of classifying any phenomena, including diseases, in terms of psychology. The 'to and fro' of the argument about whether the Wall is real or only a 'figment of the imagination' is very amusing indeed because there is a nonsensical mixture of the sublime (*a figment of the imagination*) and the trivial (*Look at the bump on my forehead*).

This contrast can be illustrated in the following way:

psychological 'theory'

imagination 	reality 
– 'a figment of the imagination' – 'Psychosomatic. You **imagined** it was there ... and imagined you hurt yourself.' – 'You **think** it does.'	– 'I walked into it' → 'bump in my forehead' – 'It still **hurts**'

funny mixture of the
SUBLIME and the TRIVIAL

At the end of this part the narrator allows himself to be drawn into the argument by describing the flying leap that someone took at the wall. The bump on the head mentioned in the previous lines develops into someone's brains being dashed out. The assumption that everything might have been a 'figment of the imagination' *apparently* has fatal consequences ('Or so it seemed'; **6** 2). This may be understood as an ironic attack on the science of psychology.

Scene 4: **6** 3–27

Wiederum liegt der Reiz der Cassette in der Variationsbreite der Stimmen. Sie ermöglichen einen schnellen Zugriff zur inhaltlichen Interpretation dieses Teils. Es geht hier um eine Umfrage zur Ergründung der Volksmeinung, in der sich die „Mauer"-Meinungen der vorhergehenden Episoden teilweise verzerrt und karikiert widerspiegeln.

1. *How do the 'islanders-in-the-street' react to the survey?*

Their answers mirror the various attitudes previously expressed about the (non-)existence of the Wall. Some of the islanders don't care, show blatant ignorance or refuse categorically to give any answer at all, while pointing out that *this* world is unpleasant enough without worrying about any other. They reject any considerations about what might be on the *other* side. Other islanders' contributions present a highly enjoyable mixture of fantastic ideas, from nihilism to dreams of paradise.

Suggestions for the blackboard:

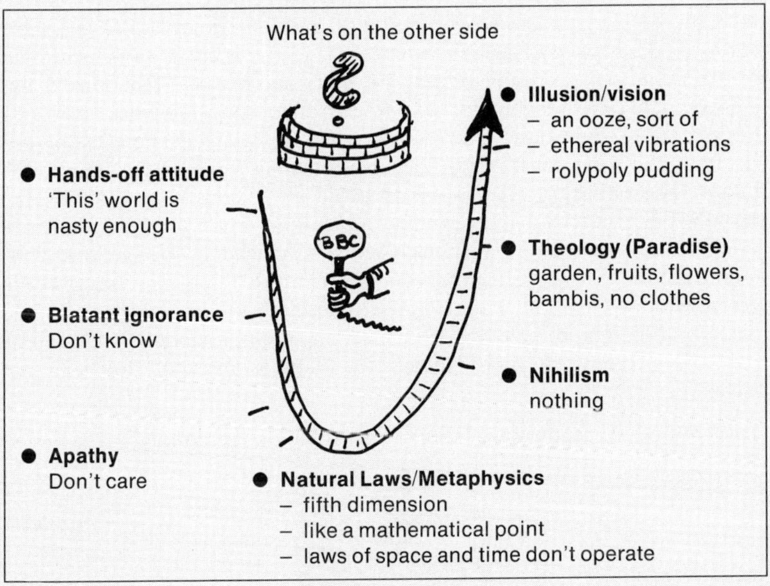

2. *Can you find comic elements?*
- The comic tension between notions like the 'mathematical point' and the infinity of space on the one hand and the 'ooze', 'the roly-poly pudding', 'bambis' and nakedness on the other hand. Again the sublime and the trivial are juxtaposed to make the audience laugh.
- The 'philosophical' attempt at giving an explanation of what is over the Wall (Voice 1, **6** 18–20).
- The narrator's final comment that summarizes the previous statements ('So there it was. Or wasn't ...'; **6** 27)

Scene 5: **6** 28–**8** 6

Der Einstieg in diesen Teil empfiehlt sich ebenfalls über das Anhören der Cassette. Die bohrenden Fragen der Kinder und die Art und Weise, wie sich die Eltern bzw. Erzieher aus der Verantwortung stehlen, sind leicht verständlich. Die Stimmführung der *voices* ermöglicht darüber hinaus gerade auch für den Teil einen raschen Zugang, in dem die verschiedenen Elternstimmen unterschiedliche Beschäftigungen vorschützen, die es ihnen nicht erlauben, auf Kinderfragen zu antworten (**7** 15–28).

1. *Why do the children ask awkward questions and how do their parents react?*
All children are characterized by a natural and sometimes almost insatiable curiosity. They keep on asking until their curiosity is either satisfied or – as in this scene – suppressed, or just not met. The parents' reactions in this episode imply that they do not want to bear the responsibility for answering their children's questions. The mother reacts aggressively and uses threats: she says she will report everything to the ruling force of the family, the father. The father, in turn, wants to avoid all responsibility. To him, the responsibility lies with the teaching authorities. They are paid, they are supposed to take on this responsibility. The teachers, however, react by telling the inquisitive child to concentrate on more 'important' things ('Said get on with my algebra'; **7** 10). Finally the father can only escape and avoid being bothered by threatening violence ('The toe of my boot'; **7** 13) and by pretending to have no time. He uses television as an excuse for being too busy.

This shifting of responsibility can be illustrated on the board:

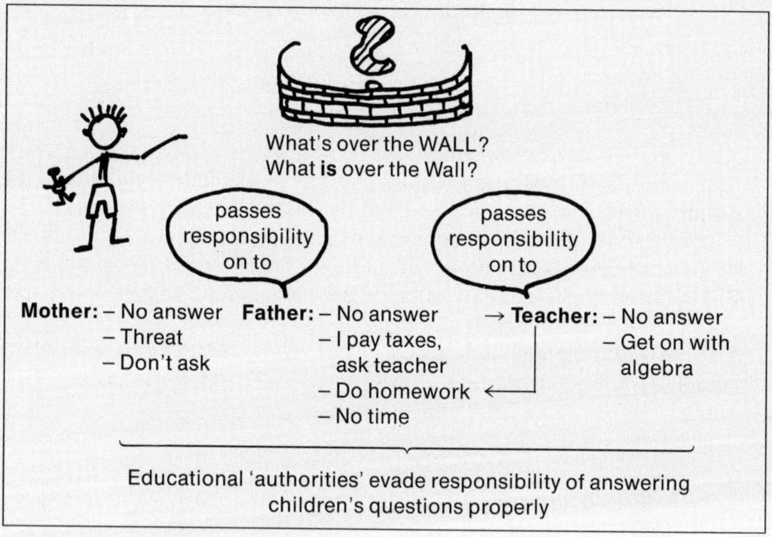

2. *How is the 'no time' theme worked out in scene 5?*
All the parents avoid their nagging children's questions. They refer to their hobbies or other activities. These activities fill their time so completely that they can be used as suitable excuses for not being able to assume any educational responsibility.

3. *What activities/hobbies are revealed in lines 15 to 28 on page 7?*
Everybody is engaged in something 'silly' or 'sensible'. The juxtaposition of very different activities has a very comic effect. The limits of space and time are deliberately broken by including one example from prehistoric times ('... to invent the wheel'; **7** 19).

The following table shows the suggested activities:

Trying to ...	No time because he/she is busy ...
watch telly/watch goldfish	– diverting him/herself
remove ferret from trousers	– going in for some crazy sport
invent wheel	– working for technological progress
cook joint	– cooking meals
bath baby	– raising children
darn socks	– looking after personal belongings
frame photo of my mother	– keeping up family bonds
write sonnet	– being creative
make a fortune	– making money
get head out	– coping with life's difficulties
bury cat	– coping with bereavement
dig a well starting at the bottom	– doing something nonsensical

4. *What role does the narrator play in this part?*
Apart from making amusing comments about what people watched in those days ('it wasn't telly'; **7** 16) the narrator uses a number of rhetorical phrases which can be regarded as a summary at the end of this part ('in short, on the whole, more or less, without splitting hairs, broadly speaking, in a nutshell'; **7** 29–30). The verbal redundancy of these lines reflects the great variety of meaningless activities put forward through the voices that speak immediately before.

After a short disagreement with one of the voices on the meaning of 'they ignored it' (**8** 1–3) the narrator introduces the idea of the 'gatecrasher' (a telling name!). In fact, the island world is compared to a party, and soon everybody descends upon the stubborn outsider.

At first, the Wall is compared to a gatecrasher ('they just ... ignored it, as you might ignore a gatecrasher at a party') and it is not until later that we realize that voice 3 has in actual fact been acting the part of a social misfit – or 'gatecrasher' – all the time, from page 7 onwards, where voice 3 takes on the role of the inquisitive child.

Unit 2: The Wall and the Gatecrasher (**8** 7–**12** 14)

Scene 6: **8** 7–30

Damit die Schüler die Fülle der Attacken auf den *gatecrasher* richtig verstehen, empfiehlt sich die Lektüre des Texts vor dem Einsatz der Cassette.

Describe the 'gatecrasher' and people's reaction to him.
The 'gatecrasher' is regarded as a rank outsider. He considers himself a rational human being and refuses to accept preconceived ideas. He wants to know more about the Wall and is angry at the islanders' indifference. The islanders react impatiently: they tell him to be humble, remind him to think of everyday reality, they recommend him not to think too much, advise him to do some sports, tell him what to do, warn him not to ask at all and finally accuse him of arrogance (**8** 29). In fact, they attack him and show their dislike of him.

Suggestions for the blackboard:

THE 'GATECRASHER'

He is ...
- not humble
- not modest
- obsessed
- arrogant
- a nuissance
- stubborn

This is what he ought to do ...
- Think of reality **here!**
- Don't think too much!
- Do something!
- Do some sports!
- Don't ask!
  (Ignorance is best.
  Leave well alone.)

The islanders attack the outsider.

Scene 7: **8** 31–**10** 26

In dieser Szene wird eine ärztliche Untersuchung parodiert. Der Text enthält viel Fachwortschatz und sollte daher vor dem Anhören der Cassette gelesen und erarbeitet werden. Die Aufnahme gestaltet stimmlich das Bedrängende der Situation und führt allmählich wie ein Crescendo zum Höhepunkt in Zeile 20/21 auf S. 10.

1. *Describe the medical check-up.*
Voice 3, the 'gatecrasher' of the previous scene, has now turned into the obstinate patient. The doctor doesn't listen to the patient at all, because he has a preconceived idea of what is wrong with him. Right at the beginning he interrupts the patient and the medical check-up begins. The audience soon find out that the relentless battery of questions is not intended to produce any medical diagnosis, but only to evade the patient's real problems and to avoid establishing any kind of genuine contact or relationship with the patient.

The questions are sometimes embarrassingly – but for the audience amusingly! – intimate ('Sex-life all right, is it? The old nudge nudge wink wink?'; **9** 12–13). After a barrage of questions covering the whole range of possible diseases and causes of illness, which end up in the last ironic question 'Got any worries, have you?' (**9** 24–**10** 10), the doctor refers his patient to a priest or a psychiatrist, gives him a grotesque prescription, calls him 'a nut' and throws him out only to begin the same procedure with a 'simpler' case.

The whole passage is meant to be a harsh ciriticism of medical procedure and includes a severe attack on theology ('They're not supposed to know, they're supposed to give comfort'; **10** 14–15) and on psychology ('He said it was my mother'; **10** 16).

2. *How does the patient react during the medical check-up?*
In the course of the medical check-up it is not the doctor who finds out about the patient's illness, but the patient himself who reveals more and more about his state of 'health'. It is not 'a bit of trouble' (**9** 1) but an 'obsession' (**9** 20).

Suggestions for the blackboard:

- a bit of trouble (**9** 1)
- All I want to know is what's on the other side (of the Wall) (**9** 7)
- I dream about walls (**9** 10)
- I wondered if there's something wrong with me (**9** 14–15)
- It's turning into a bit of … an obsession (**9** 18/20)

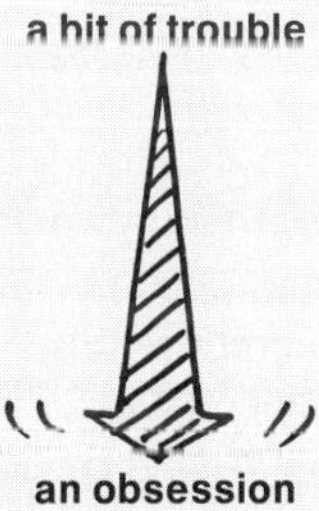

Scene 8: **10** 27–**12** 14

Die Behandlung dieses Teils kann mit dem Anhören der Cassette eröffnet werden, da der leicht zu verstehende *narrator* den Gang seiner Geschichte immer mehr bestimmt (er greift hier achtmal ein) und zu Ende führt.

1. *Describe the 'career' of the 'gatecrasher'*
The life of the 'gatecrasher' turns out to be a complete failure – including his heart attack at the end.

Suggestions for the blackboard:

The failure of the 'gatecrasher'

political attempts fail	scientific endeavours fail	social contacts fail	personal situation deteriorates
The *AFITWIOTSWOTOS* – only 1 member (himself) – is disbanded	– 30–40 years of work ↓ end in nothing	– no invitations – marriage breaks up – kids → criminals	– old – alone – penniless – skinny – threadbare

But he doesn't give up. Finally he invests his life, his own body and throws it away like a rock ('He ... sat his own skinny, threadbare old body where the rock had been'; **11** 21–23) – and catapults himself to 'the other side' (see also blackboard suggestions on p 35).

2. *How do the islanders react to the 'gatecrasher'?*
They shun him, keep away from him. On his 'Ascension Day' they are relieved to get rid of this disruptive element. They even enjoy his departure. After that they express disapproval ('shook their heads'; **12** 12) or amusement ('giggled') and return – quite content with their lot – to their work and leisure activities ('their beans, and their goldfish'; **12** 13–14).

3. *What is the function of the narrator in this part?*
The narrator becomes increasingly dominant, since we gradually receive more and more information about the end from him rather than from the 'voices'. This is to remind the audience that the play is in fact supposed to be a narration.

In addition, this enables the narrator to again view the whole world from a distance (shift of point-of-view), which is important since only he – and not the islanders – can now follow the 'gatecrasher's' flight over the Wall into infinity and tell us that 'he saw the whole gold of that sunny day' (**12** 5–6) and that it 'looked good' (**12** 8). But he doesn't answer the final question: What **is** on the other side of the Wall?

Although there are quite a number of enjoyable and ironical elements (e. g. he 'did a bit of yoga on the side'; **11** 8), the narrator's final words convey a sense of understanding. He doesn't criticize the situation. At the end there is peace.

The answers to questions 1–3 can be summed up on the board in the following way:

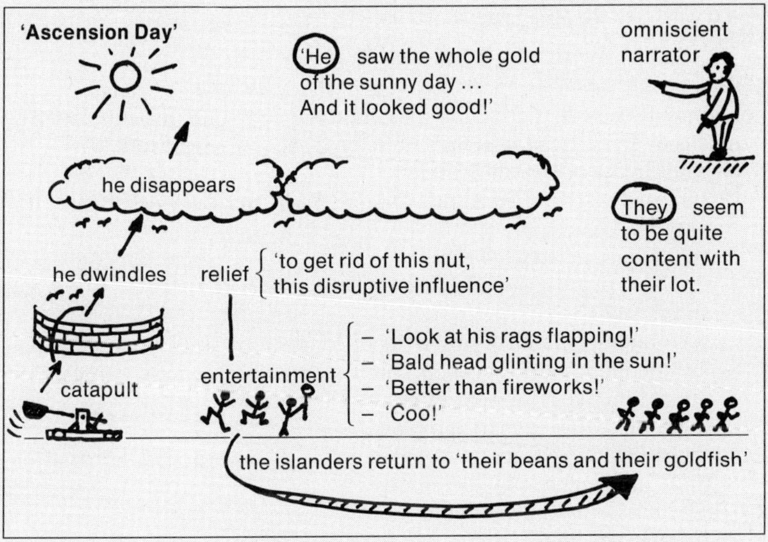

Unit 3: Further Structural and Thematic Aspects of the Play

1. *'Over the Wall' has been called a 'parable of our time'. What could be the meaning of the play?*

A parable is a (Biblical) story told to illustrate some truth. The 'truth' of *Over the Wall* might be understood as follows:

- Life in our little world (= island) is dominated and ruled by illusions, ideas, notions, and attitudes which are monopolized by a few people and turn out to be rigid mottos for our lives.
- The play is meant to make fun of all 'great' ideas by showing their relativity.
- It also shows the pettiness of the islanders, i. e. this world's people. They cannot see beyond their little world and only need 'their beans and their goldfish', i. e. they are satisfied with simple things. Anyone attempting to see **beyond** the familiarity of everyday life is regarded with suspicion, and is ultimately rejected.

- Conformity is requested and no outsiders allowed. The play throws a satirical light on this view.
- We are all on 'this side of the Wall'; only at the moment of death (once we get *Over the Wall*) will we be able to 'see'. In this respect we are all in the same boat.

2. *What could be the symbolic meaning of the 'Wall' and the 'island'?*

a) Normally a **wall** is a continuous, upright and solid structure used to enclose, divide or protect an area of land. Here it might refer to
   - walls in the history of mankind:
     Limes, Hadrian's Wall, the Chinese Wall, the Berlin Wall, the Iron Curtain, etc.
   - Individual, personal 'walls':
     diseases, death; psychological limitations such as anxieties, fears, etc.
   - social 'walls':
     surrounding and enclosing walls of conformity; walls between people and peoples; walls between families, friends, enemies, couples, relatives, etc.; general walls of non-communication
   - the 'wall' between man and God:
     the ultimate mystery of 'reality' or 'truth' forever hidden from our finite intelligence

b) The symbol of **island** could refer to
   - Britain; any community on earth in the past, present or future; life in general
     (Here a cross-reference could be made to the symbol of the island in literature: *Robinson Crusoe, Gulliver's Travels, Lord of the Flies, Utopia*, etc.)

3. *Explain the meaning of 'over' in the title of the play: '**Over** the Wall'*

'Over' here can be understood in three different ways:
- 'over' = 'about', 'on the subject of': The islanders argue/disagree *over the Wall.*
- 'over' = 'on the other side of': The 'gatescrasher' wants to know what is *over the Wall.*
- 'over' = 'to the other side of': He finally catapults himself *over the Wall.*

Further questions (for discussion/homework/group work)

4. *Discuss the difference between the terms 'humour', 'irony' and 'satire' and give examples from 'Over the Wall'.*

5. *Comment on the structure of the play: What is the function of the narrator? Why does the playwright use numbers rather than names and characters?*

6. *The 'gatecrasher' is the only one adult on the island who tries to find out what is over the Wall. Do you think his attempts heroic or silly? Would you feel sorry for him?*

7. *Consider the reactions of the islanders to the disappearance of the 'gate-crasher'. Do you respect these reactions or would you reject them?*

David Campton

Incident

Characters:

SHIRLEY ROBINSON
MISS JONES
MISS SMITH
MRS BLAKE
MISS BROWN

Scene:

The entrance hall of a hotel. It is situated in a remote village, celebrated as a beauty spot.

There are archways right and left. The right archway leads to the front entrance and dining-room. The left archway leads to the rest of the hotel – in particular to the bedrooms.

It is to be assumed that there is a fireplace to the front of the stage. To the right of the fireplace are two low easy chairs with a coffee table between them. To the left of the fireplace is a settee or settle.

At the rear is a countered cubbyhole, containing telephone and register.

SHIRLEY ROBINSON, *a friendly, bucolic, young woman, is sitting at the cubbyhole. The telephone rings. She answers it.*

SHIRLEY: Yes, this is the hotel ... The hotel ... Would you press button A? ... Yes, this is the hotel ... A room? I should think so. Single or double, Mr – er ... Smith? You did say Smith? ... It's the phone.

9	**remote** [rɪ'məʊt]	far away
11	an archway	a passage or entrance with a curved roof
14	to assume s.th. [ə'sju:m]	to suppose s.th., to take s.th. for granted
16	a settee [se'ti:]	a long sofa
	a settle	a wooden seat for two or more with a high back
17	**at the rear** [rɪə]	at the back
	a cubbyhole ['kʌbɪhəʊl]	a very small room
	countered	with a counter *(Theke)*
18	bucolic [bju:'kɒlɪk] *(lit.)*	from the country
20	press button A	In old telephone boxes the caller had to press a button to establish a connection.

Sometimes it gets out of focus. Out of –. You can't hear straight … Yes, I heard you plain enough that time, Mr Smith. But you see … The fact is … Strange as it may seem … There is no accommodation available … We haven't got a room. That is to say, we've twenty rooms, and seven baths, but they're all full … No, mister, I wouldn't pull your leg. We haven't got a room for you … Yes, I know it's out of season, but we fill up fast at the end of October. The schoolteachers, you know. Half term hols. If I were you, Mr Smith, I'd drive straight on. Don't you stop in this village at all. You have got a car? … That's a blessing, isn't it, with the rain coming on … Well, the next village is three miles one way, and four miles the other – depending on your direction. Nothing from side to side except fields and river … No, it's no use coming on spec, no matter how bad the weather is, because there won't be any room for you. Not anywhere. Not even in the hayloft … I wouldn't tell a lie, Mr Smith. There's no room for you.

(She puts the telephone down, and looks at it, half-guiltily, half-worried. Against the window comes the sudden hiss of rain.)

SHIRLEY: Oh, that old rain.

(She leaves the cubbyhole, goes to the left archway, and calls.)

SHIRLEY: Miss Brown. Miss Brown. There's just been a call. On the phone. Miss Brown …

(She goes off through the left archway. Another gust of wind and rain. Through the right archway hurry MISS JONES *and* MISS SMITH. MISS JONES *is a no-nonsense, capable person. By the side of her* MISS SMITH *seems more delicate – and considerate of other people. Both are dressed for heavy walking, and carry rucksacks. They wriggle out of their packs, and drop them by the cubbyhole.)*

1	out of focus ['fəʊkəs]	unclear (usually said of pictures) (Shirley doesn't hear Mr Smith properly.)
3	**accomodation** [əˌkɒmə'deɪʃn]	(hotel) room(s)
5	to pull s.o.'s leg	to make fun of s.o.
8	hols *(coll.)*	holidays
12	on spec *(coll.)*	on speculation; *here:* hoping to get a room without having made a reservation
14	a hayloft ['heɪlɒft]	a space under the roof of a stable or barn where hay is stored
17	a hiss	a sound like 's'
25	**considerate** [kən'sɪdərɪt]	thoughtful of the wishes, needs or feelings of others
26	They wriggle out of their packs. ['rɪgl]	They twist and struggle to take off their rucksacks.

JONES: Hallelujah! The promised land. Olde Englishe knick-knacks. I hope they include hot and cold water taps.

SMITH: Listen to that rain. We're only just in time.

JONES: Behind schedule.

SMITH: Sorry.

JONES: Can't be helped. Blisters happen to the best of us. Take your weight off 'em.

*(*MISS SMITH *limps down to the settle.)*

SMITH: It's absurd, spoiling the outing for a sore heel.

JONES: What's spoiled? We made it, didn't we? Now relax.

SMITH: I could see you panting to stride ahead. I held you back.

JONES: I said relax. Our rooms are booked here. We couldn't have gone any further.

SMITH: I couldn't ... Look – a fire. The brassware may be fake, but the fire's real.

JONES: You need a drink.

SMITH: And a hot bath. And a soft bed.

JONES: The inhabitants seem to have gone to earth. Wonder if we're disturbing their hibernation?

SMITH: I don't blame them. I could sleep as I sit here.

JONES: There ought to be a bell.

SMITH: But I mustn't, or you'll never rouse me again.

*(*MISS JONES *raps on the counter.)*

SMITH *(drowsily)*: First lesson for Arctic explorers – never go to sleep in the snow. Very practical subject, geography. At least my classes know that they must never go to sleep in the snow. Besides, I must stay awake for my bath and bed. Bed and bath. Bath and ...

1	olde, Englishe	humorous use of archaic spelling
	knickknacks ['nɪknæks]	small decorative objects
4	schedule ['ʃedju:l/'skedʒʊl]	the planned or expected time
6	**a blister**	a thin watery swelling on the skin caused e.g. by new shoes
8	**to limp**	to walk with difficulty because one foot or leg is hurt
9	**to spoil s.th.**	*here:* to destroy the pleasure of s.th.
11	**to pant** [pænt]	to breathe quickly and heavily; *here:* to be very eager
14	**brass** [brɑ:s]	*Messing*
	brassware ['brɑ:sweə]	things made of brass
	fake [feɪk]	false, imitated
19	hibernation [ˌhaɪbə'neɪʃn]	a state like a long sleep during the winter (of animals)
22	to rouse s.o. [raʊz]	to wake s.o. up
23	to rap [ræp]	to knock

JONES *(shouting)*: Shop!

SMITH: Thank you. I'm awake now.

JONES: Someone must be alive somewhere.

*(*SHIRLEY *hurries in through the left archway.)*

SHIRLEY: Have you been waiting long? I only took my eye off the place for half a minute – honestly.

JONES: Don't panic. I wrote reserving rooms.

SHIRLEY: Then you'll be Miss Jones.

JONES: The same.

SHIRLEY: We got your letter.

JONES: I'm so glad.

SHIRLEY: Two single rooms for yourself and friend.

JONES: That's what I asked for.

SHIRLEY: Two nice rooms, next to each other, looking out over the river. Not that you'll see much view tonight, you only just missed the rain. Hark at it now. Set in for the night, I should say … Oh, breakfast served from seven-thirty to nine. Actually, with only four people staying, when you want it, we get it. Would you mind signing the book?

(She pushes the register towards MISS JONES. MISS JONES *signs.)*

JONES: I take it you're not overcrowded.

SHIRLEY: Bless you, no. We've space for another twenty – not counting the annexe. That's the old boat-house done over. Folks are glad enough to sleep anywhere when the season's on. Come in hundreds, they do, poor dears, to see a bit of unspoiled England. You should see the car park in season. Room for a hundred cars we've got. Not just for the guests of course: there's the dining room. Only the season's over now. Only two other guests. One passing through, like you, and one permanent for the time being.

JONES: Permanent?

SHIRLEY: There are special rates for permanents out of season. She …

(She stops as MRS BLAKE *appears in the left archway. She is an elderly lady with a piercing eye. There is a slight pause as she studies the group at the desk.)*

JONES: Evening.

15	hark! [hɑːk] *(archaic or dialectal)*	listen!
22	an annexe ['æneks]	a smaller building added to a larger one, e.g. a hotel or school
	to do s.th. over	to redecorate (a room)

(After a slight nod, MRS BLAKE *turns brusquely, and goes to the settle. She is a little taken aback to find* MISS SMITH *there.* MISS SMITH *appears to have dozed off.* MRS BLAKE *goes over to one of the chairs by the coffee table.)*

SHIRLEY *(in a hoarse whisper)*: Mrs Blake.

BLAKE: Thank you, Miss Robinson. I am quite capable of introducing myself. Should the need arise.

SHIRLEY: Would you ask your friend to sign? Looks like she's dropped off.

JONES: Dora ... Dora!

SMITH *(opening her eyes)*: I heard every word. *(She notices* MRS BLAKE.*)* Oh ... Good evening.

*(*MRS BLAKE *nods silently.)*

JONES *(holding out the pen)*: Will you?

SMITH: Will I? ... Oh – of course.

(She limps to the desk.)

SHIRLEY: Have you damaged yourself?

SMITH: A blister.

SHIRLEY: Blister! They're wicked things. Just you look after it. Would you like me to find a bandage?

SMITH *(signing the register)*: I have a tin of Elastoplast, thank you.

SHIRLEY: You been walking far?

JONES: A mere twenty-fives miles today.

SHIRLEY: Poor lamb. No wonder you're worn out.

SMITH *(putting down the pen)*: There.

SHIRLEY: That's right. I'll carry your pack. You take care of that blister Miss ...

(She glances at the register. Her smile fades. She puts down the pack. There is a pause as she stares at MISS SMITH.)

BLAKE *(suddenly breaking the silence)*: Another?

SMITH: What's the matter? Have I made a mistake?

*(*MISS JONES *looks at the register.)*

SHIRLEY: You didn't say.

JONES: Perfectly legible.

1	brusque [bru:sk/brʌsk]	abrupt and rather impolite
2	to be taken aback [ə'bæk]	to be surprised or shocked
3	**to doze off** [dəʊz]	to fall into a light sleep
4	**hoarse** [hɔ:s]	rough-sounding
7	to drop off	to fall into a light sleep
17	**wicked** ['wɪkɪd]	extremely bad, nasty
19	Elastoplast [ɪ'læstəplɑ:st]	adhesive dressing for wounds *(Wundpflaster)*
32	**legible** ['ledʒəbl]	clear enough to be read

SHIRLEY: You didn't say in your letter.

JONES: I said all that needed to be said. Two single ladies require two single rooms. What more do you want – banker's references?

SHIRLEY: But how was I to know? I can't tell by just looking. What am I to do now?

JONES: You're to show us upstairs. I'm waiting for a wash.

SHIRLEY: I'm not sure that – that ... I mean, if I hadn't already ... I'll have to ask you to wait here for a minute. While I fetch Miss Brown.

JONES: Can't *she* – wait?

SHIRLEY: Miss Brown's the manager. But she can't blame me. I wasn't told. You didn't say, did you?

SMITH: But what's the matter?

SHIRLEY: If only you'd said!

(She scurries out through the left archway.)

JONES: Part of the bucolic atmosphere. It goes with the cardboard panelling and phoney beams.

SMITH: I could have done without it tonight. I'm cold.

JONES: Come back to the fire.

SMITH: This isn't such a friendly place. It's cold. For all the Olde Englishe trappings, it's cold. I wish we could have gone on.

JONES: Another three miles? You'd have been a stretcher case by then ... I'm glad the girl went for the manager, though. It saves me the trouble of sending for her.

(As they come down to the fire, they realize that MRS BLAKE *is still staring at them. The intensity of her gaze makes them uncomfortable.* MISS SMITH *sits nervously on the settle.* MISS JONES *stands firmly in front of the fire, as though defying anyone to move her.)*

JONES *(to* MRS BLAKE*)*: Turned nasty, hasn't it?

3	a banker's reference ['refrəns]	a note from one's bank saying that one is a trustworthy customer
14	to scurry ['skʌrɪ]	to hurry; to walk with quick, short steps
15	panelling ['pænəlɪŋ]	boards (usually of wood) covering the walls of a room
	cardboard ['kɑ:dbɔ:d]	a stiff brownish material like thick paper
16	phoney ['fəʊnɪ]	fake, false
	a beam [bi:m]	a thick bar of wood supporting the ceiling or roof
20	trappings ['træpɪŋz]	décor
21	**a stretcher** ['stretʃə]	a covered frame on which a sick person can be carried by two people
25	**a gaze** [geɪz]	a stare, a long, fixed look
27	to defy s.o. to do s.th. [dɪ'faɪ]	to make it quite clear that it's no use trying to do s.th.

(There is no reply – merely a continuation of the close scrutiny.)

JONES: After a very promising start to the day. *(Pause.)* Still, it may clear up before morning. *(Pause. She is becoming irritated by* MRS BLAKE'S *refusal to speak.)* A shallow depression is moving rapidly north-east. Storms are expected in all areas. Temperatures will be sub-normal, with frost on high ground.

SMITH *(reprovingly)*: Molly!

(Slight pause.)

JONES: Walked twenty-five miles today ... For the hell of it ... Half term, and all that. Schoolteachers, you know. My name's Jones. My friend ...

BLAKE: It happens regularly. They don't realize ...

JONES: Who don't?

SMITH: We hardly expected the Savoy or Claridges. And the receptionist was very friendly. She offered to find a bandage. The receptionist at the Savoy or Claridges wouldn't have offered to find a bandage. That is ... Not without ... Without ...

*(*MRS BLAKE *sits in an attitude which plainly suggests that she is not listening.* MISS SMITH *falters, and lapses into silence.)*

JONES: My friend spoke to you.

BLAKE: They don't realize.

JONES: You're a resident here.

BLAKE: So you were informed.

JONES: Anything wrong with that girl at the desk?

BLAKE: She follows instructions.

JONES: What might they be?

BLAKE: You must ask the manager.

SMITH *(hastily, before* MISS JONES *has a chance to lose her temper)*: Of course there must be a misunderstanding. The booking was confirmed weeks ago. *(She pauses, baffled by the lack of response from* MRS BLAKE.*)*

1	**scrutiny** ['skru:tɪnɪ]	a careful examination
3	**to irritate s.o.** ['ɪrɪteɪt]	to make s.o. angry or impatient
4	a depression	(in weather forecasts) an area of low atmospheric pressure
7	to reprove s.o. [rɪ'pru:v]	to speak disapprovingly of s.o., to scold s.o.
9	for the hell of it	just for fun
18	to falter ['fɔ:ltə]	to hesitate, to stammer
	to lapse into silence [læps]	to fall silent, to stop speaking
21	**a resident** ['rezɪdənt]	s.o. who lives in a certain place or area
29	baffled ['bæfld]	having difficulty in understanding, bewildered, puzzled

After all, we are in England. *(She falters, then presses on.)* Have you ever travelled abroad, Mrs … *(She gives up.)*

BLAKE: I am deaf in one ear. I am blind in one eye.

SMITH *(sincerely)*: I'm so sorry!

BLAKE: I see what I want to see. I hear what I want to hear.

JONES: Now, listen …

*(*MISS BROWN *enters through the left archway. She wears an almost permanent smile. She speaks correctly, but rather like someone who has learned to speak that way.* SHIRLEY *enters behind her.)*

BROWN: Good evening.

JONES *(turning to face her)*: The manager?

BROWN: Miss Brown … I believe there has been a slight difficulty.

JONES: None that I know of. Presumably your staff mistook …

BROWN: One moment please. Excuse me. *(She examines the register.)* Ah, yes … Miss Smith.

SMITH *(rising)*: Yes?

BLAKE: Ah!

BROWN: Most unfortunate. I hope you will accept our sincere apologies.

JONES: Put that way, who are we to refuse?

BROWN: Your letter misled us, of course. You made no mention of a Miss Smith.

JONES: I said Miss Jones and friend.

BROWN: But not – Miss Smith.

JONES: My mistake. Now that piece of red tape has been tied up, perhaps I can see my room.

BROWN: Miss Robinson, will you show this lady to her room.

SHIRLEY: Which – luggage is yours, Miss Jones?

JONES: It doesn't matter. They're both going up.

BROWN: I'm afraid not.

JONES: Not?

BROWN: That is why I apologized. We have a reputation for hospitality.

SMITH: Then where is my room?

BROWN: A clerical error. Most regrettable. No room was reserved for you.

JONES: Nonsense. I booked 'em. For Jones and friend.

BROWN: But not for Miss Smith. We didn't reserve that room for Miss Smith.

13	**presumably** [prɪ'zju:məblɪ]	probably; it is to be presumed or supposed
20	**to mislead s.o.** [mɪs'li:d]	to give s.o. a wrong idea of s.th.
24	red tape [ˌ–'–]	unnecessary official rules that delay action
33	a clerical error ['klerɪkəl]	a mistake in the office books

SMITH: It doesn't matter. I'll be satisfied with any other room.

BROWN: Ah, there's the pity. We have no other room. I'm sure you'll find another hotel. One able to accommodate you.

JONES: Oh, talk sense.

BROWN: I hoped I had made the situation quite clear.

JONES: That you refuse to …

BROWN: That the hotel is quite full.

JONES: You should keep your staff in the picture. She told us that you were empty.

SHIRLEY: But they didn't say.

BROWN: Shirley, you may go.

SHIRLEY: Yes, Miss Brown.

JONES: Disposing of the evidence? You stay here … I said stay.

BROWN: I accept all responsibility. I am in full control here.

JONES: You refused. That's the situation, isn't it? My friend Miss Smith … You refused to …

BROWN: I haven't said so.

JONES: Then say it now.

BLAKE: Yes.

SMITH: I don't believe it.

(She goes to a chair by the coffee table.)

SMITH: I don't …

(She sits. As she does so, MRS BLAKE *gets up.)*

BLAKE: Excuse me.

(She crosses to the settle, and sits. There is a slight, shocked pause.)

BLAKE: One has principles. Not that I hold anything against the young woman personally. She may be a sweet girl, devoted to her parents, and fond of animals. But a line must be drawn somewhere.

JONES: Will someone translate?

BLAKE: The gesture was melodramatic, I admit. But now you understand the position of the manager. She has others to consider.

SMITH: Suddenly I'm untouchable?

BLAKE: It's a question of standards. Other hotels are not so particular. Forgive my speaking so bluntly: I've no wish to hurt anyone.

JONES: I'm allowed, but she's not. Where's the logic? Where's the difference between us? Miss Brown, the manager …

4	to talk sense	to talk reasonably, logically
13	to dispose of s.th. [dɪˈspəʊz]	to get rid of s.th.
34	**blunt** [blʌnt]	plain, frank, not trying to be polite

BROWN: We are always open. Winter and summer. To anyone. With absolutely no discrimination. We have a reputation. But when the hotel is full, what more is there to say?

JONES: Would you recognize a lie if you saw it face to face?

BROWN: Please accept the situation. Feelings can be hurt so easily.

JONES: Do I have to shout to make myself understood? Why?

BLAKE: As if it weren't obvious. She is a . . . a . . . *(She struggles with a word which is obviously distasteful.)* A Smith!

JONES: A what?

BLAKE: You can hardly expect me to repeat the word.

SMITH: My name? Because of my name you refuse to . . .

BROWN: I have never refused. I made that quite clear.

JONES: I'm losing my grip on reality. You're not real. You're only delirium – a touch of fever. A couple of aspirins, and a good night's rest, and you'll vanish.

SMITH: But my name's only a word – a sound. Smith.

BLAKE: Ugh.

SMITH: Smith. What does that mean? Nothing. Except that my father's name was Smith.

BLAKE: It runs in the blood. A Smith is a Smith, and you can't get away from it.

SMITH: I never wanted to.

BLAKE: The arrogance of the tribe!

JONES: Since when have Smiths been untouchable?

BROWN: There's nothing to be gained by an inquisition.

JONES: You there.

SHIRLEY: Me?

JONES: What does the name Smith mean to you?

SHIRLEY: I'd rather not say, miss.

JONES: Why not?

SHIRLEY: I was always told it wasn't very nice.

JONES: Told? What were you told?

SHIRLEY: I'd rather not say.

JONES: Why?

7	**obvious** [ˈɒbvɪəs]	evident, easy to see, clear
8	**distasteful** [dɪsˈteɪstfʊl]	unpleasant, disgusting
13	delirium [dɪˈlɪərɪəm]	disturbed state of mind when one has a fever
15	**to vanish** [ˈvænɪʃ]	to disappear
23	**a tribe** [traɪb]	a group of people of the same race; family, clan
25	**an inquisition** [ˌɪnkwɪˈzɪʃən]	a long, official interrogation

SHIRLEY: Because it's not very nice.

BLAKE: Have you ever consulted a telephone directory? Have you ever looked at the pages devoted to Smiths? Have you ever considered how they outnumber the rest of us? Think it over some time. When you've thought long enough, you'll realize why some of us are concerned. They're a powerful group – the Smiths.

SMITH: You're afraid – of me?

SHIRLEY: When I was a little girl, I was told never to play with the boys in the next yard. They weren't our sort. They were taken away in the end, and I never heard what happened to them. Their name was Smith, I think. At least, when I think of Smiths, I think of them.

BLAKE: Everywhere one turns, one meets them. They crawl through our daily life like an unmentionable disease.

SHIRLEY: I was always told that if I wasn't a good girl, the Smiths would come for me.

BLAKE: There are Smiths in the law, Smiths in medicine, Smiths in politics, Smiths in the church, Smiths in the army, navy, and air force, in the police, in the prisons, in the Commons, in the Lords, Smiths in the BBC...

SHIRLEY: I was always told never to trust a Smith. They'll do you down as soon as look at you.

BLAKE: Commerce is riddled with them – W. H. Smith, Smith's Clocks, Smith's Crisps ...

SHIRLEY: I was always told that Smiths never use a handkerchief.

BLAKE: Make no mistake: Smiths are a menace to the English way of life.

SMITH *(jumping up)*: Stop it. Stop it!

SHIRLEY: I was told they ought never to have been let in the country in the first place.

BROWN: That will do, Miss Robinson.

SHIRLEY: Yes, Miss Brown. *(Turns to go.)*

BROWN *(to* MISS JONES*)*: With your permission of course.

(She nods to SHIRLEY, *who goes.)*

4	**to outnumber s.o.** [aʊt'nʌmbə]	be more in numbers than s.o.
13	**a disease** [dɪ'zi:z]	an illness
20	to do s.o. down	to speak negatively about s.o., to degrade s.o.
	as soon as	*here:* with the same willingness as
22	to be riddled with ['rɪdld]	to be full of (s.th. undesirable)
25	**a menace** ['menɪs]	a threat, a danger
27	in the first place	to begin with, at all

JONES: She makes me ashamed of being a teacher. 'I was told'. If we can't teach them to think for themselves, what's the use of trying to teach anything?

SMITH: She did offer to find a bandage.

BROWN: Will you be taking your pack now?

*(*MISS SMITH *limps over to* MRS BLAKE. MRS BLAKE *shrinks to the end of the settle.)*

SMITH: Why should you want to hurt me?

BLAKE: Typical. Typical.

SMITH: I never hurt anyone knowingly.

BLAKE: Kindly stop molesting me.

SMITH: We're human. Two eyes, two arms, two legs, one head, one heart. What else matters?

BLAKE: The government ought to take a stand. It would if it weren't corrupted from within. Whitehall is riddled with Smiths.

SMITH: What harm have I ever done to you?

BLAKE: You? Your crew! … When my husband died, I was provided for. We had both been careful: our generation was taught the value of thrift. We had prepared for a quiet old age. Even without him, life offered compensations; a small place of my own, with a garden, maybe – not so large as to be a burden, but enough to show the changing seasons. For the rest – books, firelight, and muffins for tea. It was provided for, in safe investments. The money was there. Only it wasn't quite enough. A few years ago perhaps … But now – dear me, no. The price of property, the cost of domestic help … The money is still there – on paper. But year by year, the figures mean less and less. And here I am, with no place of my own: only a hotel with special rates for permanents out of season: and in the summer, a top back room, with no running water. Why here? you may ask. Why not South Kensington or Bournemouth with the rest of the

6	**to shrink** [ʃrɪŋk]	to become smaller; *here:* to move away from s.th. unpleasant
11	to molest s.o. [mə'lest]	to disturb and annoy s.o.
17	**a crew** [kru:]	a group of people working together *(Mannschaft); here:* any group of people
18	thrift [θrɪft]	wise and careful use of money
20	**a compensation** [ˌkɒmpen'seɪʃn]	something offered to make up for a damage or loss
22	muffins ['mʌfɪnz]	small, round breadlike cakes usually eaten hot with butter
24	property ['prɒpətɪ]	*here:* houses

flock? I'm not a beggar: I prefer not to display my sores. But each year the money buys less and less. And what is the forecast for the year after next? A charitable institution for faded gentlewomen? ... Who tainted the money? Who stole my Indian Summer?

SMITH: You poor dear ...

(She stretches out her hand to MRS BLAKE. MRS BLAKE *shrinks from her.)*

SMITH: Why shrink from me?

BLAKE: You smell.

*(*MISS SMITH *recoils with a cry.* MRS BLAKE, *slightly embarrassed by her outburst, crosses to the coffee table.)*

BLAKE: I can smell out a Smith anywhere.

*(*MISS SMITH, *struggling to keep her composure, hurries across the room as well as she can, and picks up her pack.* MISS JONES *catches her arm.)*

JONES: Where do you think you're off to?

SMITH: Let me go.

JONES: How can you go like that?

SMITH: If I stay, I'll end by believing them.

JONES: You're not leaving them the last word. *(Urges* MISS SMITH *back to the settle.)* You've been walking all day, remember? You're not splashing through the dark for three more miles.

BROWN: But if there's no alternative?

JONES: There is. Here.

SMITH: What they believe is twisted, but they believe it. They believe that I – that I ...

JONES: You're not. Now will you sit, or do I have to make you?

BLAKE: I warn the management that I could not possibly stay in a place that harbours a Smith. No matter how favourable the out-of-season rates ... Smiths! I've seen them in their long, shiny cars. Where does all that

1	a flock [flɒk]	a large group of animals or people
	a sore [sɔ:]	a wound, a painful place on the body
3	**charitable** ['tʃærɪtəbl]	helping people in need
	to fade	to lose strength and freshness
	to taint s.th. [teɪnt]	to spoil s.th.
4	**Indian summer**	a period of warm weather in the autumn
9	to recoil	to move quickly away from s.th. unpleasant
12	**composure** [kəm'pəʊʒə]	calmness
14	Where are you off to?	Where are you going?
19	to splash [splæʃ]	*here:* to walk through puddles *(Pfützen)*
23	to twist s.th. [twɪst]	to bend s.th.; *here:* to change the true meaning of s.th.
27	to harbour s.o.	to give shelter to s.o., to protect s.o.

money come from, eh? How can they afford long, shiny cars when I wear the same coat year after year?

SMITH: Please, Molly.

BLAKE: Vice.

JONES: Sit.

*(*MISS SMITH *sits.)*

BROWN: Can't you let well alone?

JONES: That would suit you fine, wouldn't it? You nearly won. She was on her way out.

BROWN *(still smiling)*: I have an establishment to run.

JONES: You have me to deal with. Me. You want a fight? Right. Let's get on with it.

BROWN: I have to consider what is best for everyone. Even though that may call for the occasional sacrifice.

JONES: Smile as much as you like; but you're not sacrificing her. *We* shall leave when *we* planned. Tomorrow morning.

BLAKE: You are aware of my ultimatum, Miss Brown?

BROWN: Miss Jones, you're not even aware of my problem. Why should you be? Backstairs business is no concern of the guests. But this hotel has a standard. Not many years ago this place was considered a den of iniquity, tucked away from the main road. Even the villagers preferred the other inns – three miles in one direction, and four in the other. Then I took over. Now we accommodate a hundred cars at the height of the season. I made this place what it is ... I smile, Miss Jones, partly because it is my nature to smile, and partly because a person in my position is expected to smile. But you mustn't mistake my smile for a weakness. I am quite equal to a trial of strength. I say there is no accommodation available for Miss Smith.

*(*MISS SMITH *stands.)*

JONES: Sit down. Where's your self-respect?

SMITH: I don't think Smiths are allowed self-respect. They either crawl

4	**vice** [vaɪs]	evil, immoral behaviour; bad habit
7	to let well alone	to make no change to s.th. that is satisfactory
14	**a sacrifice** ['sækrɪfaɪs]	s.th. one gives up which one wants to keep or do *(Opfer)*
19	backstairs ['bæksteəz]	*here:* behind the scenes (of a hotel)
20	a den of iniquity [den, ɪ'nɪkwɪtɪ]	a place of wickedness or crime
21	to tuck s.th. away [tʌk]	to hide s.th.
27	a trial ['traɪəl]	*here:* a test

away, or sit back while others fight for them. Neither course is good for one's self-respect.

JONES: Then fight with me.

BROWN: There'll be no battle … Let me tell you something else – purely personal, but not irrelevant. I was brought up in Stepney. My family lived in two rooms. You wouldn't have guessed? I wouldn't have mentioned it; but you must realize that I also know what it means to fight.

JONES: I'm not retreating.

BROWN: I didn't suppose you would.

JONES: The weather's filthy, and she's lame. You'll turn her out limping. Can't you be shamed?

BLAKE: She'll find another Smith somewhere. They always do. They cling together. Are you sure you're a Jones?

BROWN: Is the foot very painful?

SMITH: I have a tin of Elastoplast.

JONES: And what's another mile after twenty-five? What if she doesn't quite make it to the next village? What's a wet night under a hedge? Nothing to concern you. You'll have done your duty by popular prejudice.

BROWN: Will you be able to walk another three miles?

SMITH: I don't know till I try.

JONES: I won't let you all forget this evening in a hurry.

BROWN: I told you there was no room for Miss Smith in this hotel.

BLAKE: There's no room for a Smith anywhere. We're better off without them. They're responsible for … They're responsible.

BROWN: However …

BLAKE: You're not weakening?

BROWN: We may be able to reach a compromise.

SMITH: Compromise?

BLAKE: What did you say?

BROWN: Compromise.

JONES: What does that mean?

BROWN: We have the annexe.

SMITH: The annexe?

5	Stepney ['stepnɪ]	district of East London
8	**to retreat**	to move back, giving up a fight
12	**to cling to s.o.** [klɪŋ]	to stay very close to s.o.
18	by	*here:* according to; from the point of view of
	prejudice ['predʒədɪs]	an opinion (esp. a dislike of a certain group of people) not based on reason

BROWN: It used to be the boathouse – on the far side of the grounds. I had it converted. It is waterproof and draught-proof.

JONES: I see. Or think I see.

BROWN: It is used in the season for our overflow. It hasn't quite the amenities of the hotel, but it provides a useful second best.

JONES: Second best?

BROWN: But all our guests receive full attention. You could have your breakfast brought to your room. For the sake of the other guests, such as Mrs Blake, I would prefer you not to use the dining-room.

JONES: Naturally they must be considered.

BROWN: I am making an effort. Aren't you willing to meet me half way?

JONES: It's a compromise.

BROWN: It's a solution.

BLAKE: It's the thin end of the wedge.

BROWN: Do you object?

BLAKE: The only good Smith is a dead Smith. However, I wouldn't want the girl to catch pneumonia.

BROWN: Miss Jones? Shall I have a bed made up over there?

JONES: Two beds. We stick together.

BROWN: Thank you. I'll show the way. Don't bother about the packs: I'll have them brought straight over. We can pick up an umbrella on the way out. *(She leads the way to the left archway.)* Will you come this way, Miss Smith?

SMITH: No.

BROWN: I beg your pardon?

SMITH: I'm afraid I had to say no.

BROWN: But we've just come to an agreement.

SMITH: My friend agreed. I didn't.

JONES: Dora!

SMITH: Sorry, Molly. But I do have a mind of my own.

BLAKE: You see. You see. Typical.

SMITH: I cannot take your second best.

2	**to convert s.th.** [kən'vɜ:t]	to change s.th. so that it fulfills a different purpose
	waterproof ['– – –]	which cannot be penetrated by water
	a draught [drɑ:ft]	a current of cold air
5	**amenities** [ə'mi:nɪtɪz]	things (in a hotel) that help to make one's stay pleasant
14	the thin end of the wedge [wedʒ]	an event or action that seems unimportant but is likely to lead to others that are much more serious
17	**pneumonia** [nju:'məʊnɪə]	an inflammation of the lungs

BROWN: I don't think you understand. There is no room in the hotel, but I am offering alternative accommodation.

SMITH: And I am declining. It was a kind gesture: I appreciate what it must have cost you – after all, you have to live here with your permanent guests.

BROWN: The annexe is very comfortable. We've never had a complaint.

SMITH: I'm sure of that. But it's the division, you see. Sheep from goats. I can't agree with that.

JONES: But I'm coming with you. We're friends.

SMITH: Some of my best friends are Smiths.

JONES: That was uncalled for.

SMITH: Do I sound ungrateful? I'm sorry. I don't mean to be. But I have no intention of accepting the second-class label. I can be turned out into the wet, but I cannot be forced into accepting your second-rate accommodation.

BROWN: In the season, guests are very glad to take it.

SMITH: So should I be – in the season. It's not the place, it's the division. It would be just the same if everyone moved into the annexe, and I was left in the hotel. That would mean accepting a difference between us. There is no difference. If I took up your kind offer, I'd be agreeing with you. I can't agree with you.

JONES: It's still raining.

BROWN: I went as far as I dared.

SMITH: I'm sorry. It wasn't enough.

BLAKE: Give them an inch, and they grab the rest.

JONES: Don't be a fool, Dora, I've just settled everything.

SMITH: Please don't be angry, Molly. It isn't worth it.

3	to decline [dɪ'klaɪn]	to refuse an offer
	to appreciate s.th. [ə'pri:ʃɪeɪt]	to acknowledge s.th., to understand s.th.
7	**a goat** [gəʊt]	*Ziege*
11	uncalled for	not necessary, not wanted
13	**a label** ['leɪbl]	a tag; a piece of paper, cloth or metal on an object describing its nature; *here:* a classification
14	second-rate	second-class, of inferior quality
25	**to grab s.th.**	to take s.th. quickly and with force

JONES: Why dig in your heels? You sat meek and mild while that old bitch piled on the insults.

SMITH: Perhaps the last insult was one too many.

JONES: I won a point. They've never had a Smith, even in the annexe before. Are you telling me I might have saved my breath?

SMITH: You said some very noble things.

JONES: It won't be so easy again. They'll say 'All alike those Smiths. Do them a favour, and they throw it back in your face. Remember last time.' And they'll mean you.

SMITH: You said I had to keep my self-respect.

JONES: I'm keeping you out of the wet. You're too tired to think straight. Get the keys, Miss Brown. We're coming over.

SMITH: You may. I'm not.

JONES: I've never seen you so pig-headed before.

SMITH: I've never been in this situation before.

BLAKE: They never give way. Top dogs or nothing.

JONES: Everyone is being reasonable now.

SMITH: I'm only doing what I have to do.

JONES: Can't you be reasonable? What more do you expect me to do for you – join you in a ditch?

SMITH: You'll do what you have to do.

JONES: I've smoothed everything out.

SMITH: Yes. It's all so easy now. I could slide down so comfortably. I only have to agree.

JONES *(angrily)*: I did my best, but it wasn't enough. Throw that in my face. All or nothing. That's your attitude.

SMITH *(mildly)*: Yes.

JONES: You won't get it. Nobody ever gets that.

SMITH: You can't force me to give way, Molly. You wouldn't want to.

1	**heel** [hi:l]	back part of the foot
	to dig in one's heels	to refuse to move or do what others want
	meek [mi:k]	gentle and uncomplaining
	a bitch *(sl.)*	a nasty woman
2	to pile on [paɪl]	to add a lot to a pile or heap
	an insult [ˈɪnsʌlt]	an offensive remark
14	pig-headed	stubborn; holding to an opinion in spite of reason
16	top dog *(sl.)* [ˌ–ˈ–]	person in the highest position
20	**a ditch** [dɪtʃ]	a long narrow channel at the side of the road *(Graben)*
22	to smooth s.th. out [smu:ð]	*here:* to remove problems and difficulties

JONES: Are you leaving me to their sniggers? At least think of me.

SMITH: I hadn't thought of that.

JONES *(with irony)*: Naturally.

SMITH: I – I …

*(*SHIRLEY *hurries in through the left archway.)*

SHIRLEY: Miss Brown, I …

BROWN: Sssh!

JONES: Well?

SMITH: Miss Brown, is there room for me here among your other guests – for me, Miss Smith?

BROWN: Please don't ask.

SMITH: Goodnight. *(Picks up her pack.)*

JONES *(losing her temper)*: Go out into the downpour, then. Get drowned.

SMITH: Are we still friends?

JONES: Fool. Fool. Fool.

SMITH: Maybe. *(She limps out through the right archway.)*

JONES *(shouting after her)*: I don't care. Get that clear. Do what the hell you like. Only don't make me look a clown again. I tell you, I just don't care. *(She stands, panting, as the outburst passes. She looks around at the others staring at her. The situation once more ceases to be a personal disagreement with* MISS SMITH.*)*

JONES *(to herself)*: Dora. *(She turns, and dashes out through the right archway, calling.)* Dora. Dora. Dora!

(Slight pause.)

BROWN: You were about to say, Shirley?

SHIRLEY: I was wondering about the old boathouse.

BROWN: There's no need.

SHIRLEY: I didn't suppose so.

BROWN: Smith. It's a pity.

SHIRLEY: Something ought to be done about them.

BROWN: What do you suggest?

SHIRLEY: I don't know. Something. They're not like us.

BROWN: In what way?

SHIRLEY: Well, they're Smiths.

BLAKE: Dinner is now being served, I take it?

1	sniggers ['snɪgəz]	half-suppressed, unpleasant laughter
13	downpour ['daʊnpɔ:]	heavy fall of rain
20	**to cease** [si:s]	to stop
22	**to dash** [dæʃ]	to run quickly, to rush
35	I take it	I suppose

(She moves towards the right archway where she meets MISS JONES *returning.* MISS JONES *is subdued.)*

JONES: Don't go ... By the time I reached the door, she was out of sight. It's almost black outside – the rain drives into your face. I couldn't even tell which way she took – whether she went forward or back. I think she'd go forward.

SHIRLEY: I hope she'll be all right by the river.

JONES: You're not the only one. *(As* MRS BLAKE *makes a movement.)* Please don't go ... We never disagreed on anything that mattered. How could we? We were friends.

*(*MRS BLAKE *moves towards the archway again.)*

BLAKE: Excuse me.

JONES: I said don't go.

BLAKE: I am not accustomed to taking orders.

JONES: How nice for you.

BROWN: I must ask you to remember where you are.

JONES: Am I likely to forget? How did it happen?

BROWN: What?

JONES: How did I end on your side? I don't remember crossing over. What am I doing here with your crew, Mrs Blake?

*(*MRS BLAKE *turns away with a look of patient resignation.)*

JONES: Yes, you. Poor, scared, old lady. If I didn't despise you, I'd be sorry for you.

BROWN: Miss Jones ...

JONES: You don't know what's going to happen to you, and you're frightened. That's all. There's something nasty waiting round the corner, and who's to blame for that?

BLAKE: I don't have to listen.

JONES: Yes, you do ... The villains can't be people like us. So let's – smell out – the people not like us – the people with funny-shaped noses, and odd ears, and the wrong-sized boots. If only you could get rid of every one of them, you might be safe. It's pathetic. You're afraid, that's all.

BLAKE: Miss Brown ...

BROWN: That is quite sufficient.

2	subdued [səb'dju:d]	unusually quiet
22	**scared** [skeəd]	frightened, full of fear
	to despise s.o. [dɪ'spaɪz]	to regard s.o. as worthless, to look down on s.o.
29	**a villain** ['vɪlən]	a wicked, evil person (e.g. in a novel or play)
32	pathetic [pə'θetɪk]	*here:* lamentable, contemptible

JONES: But you're worse, Miss Brown, the manager. You know better, but still you join in the hunt.

BROWN: I said, that is enough.

JONES: In control, you say? You crawl. The Blakes of this world stand between you and that slum in Stepney, so you crawl to them. Aren't you ashamed?

BROWN: I –

JONES: I am. Because here I am, too – on your side. I agreed that she wasn't one of us. I hate myself.

BLAKE: That doesn't surprise me.

JONES: But who comes next? There'll always be somebody under the axe. When they're finished off, whose turn will it be then? Cockneys? School-teachers? Ladies over sixty?

BROWN: I take it you won't be staying here tonight.

JONES: I'm following her. It's a futile gesture: I may be blundering in the wrong direction. But I have to do something to – to ... I let down the human race. *(She picks up her pack.)* Goodbye. Sleep well.

(She goes out.)

BLAKE: Uncouth. You're not firm enough, Miss Brown. After all, you are in control. A no is a no, and after that one calls for the constable. I was merely on my way to dinner, and I was made to feel uncomfortable. Ladies over sixty indeed! You must take a firm line in future, Miss Brown. *(She sweeps grandly to the right archway.)*

BROWN *(sotto voce)*: Oh, go to hell.

BLAKE: I beg your pardon?

BROWN: I said – very well, Mrs Blake.

BLAKE: I should hope so. *(She goes out through the right archway.* MISS BROWN *turns, and sees* SHIRLEY *staring at her.)*

BROWN: If you can't find anything better to do, then look until you can.

SHIRLEY: Yes, Miss Brown. *(She hurries out through the left archway.)*

BROWN: Remember I am in control here. *(She realizes that her hand is resting on the open register.)* In complete control.

(She slams the register shut.)

11	**an axe** [æks]	a tool used for cutting wood
12	a Cockney ['kɒknɪ]	a person born in the East End of London
15	futile ['fju:taɪl]	useless, having no effect
	to blunder ['blʌndə]	*here:* to move unsteadily (as if blind)
16	to let s.o. down	to disappoint s.o. who relied on one's help
19	uncouth [ʌn'ku:θ]	having bad manners, impolite
20	constable ['kʌnstəbl]	policeman

David Campton acting in one of his plays

By courtesy of J. Garnet Miller Ltd.

Biographical Notes

David Campton was born in Leicester in 1924. In 1941 he took a job as a clerk with the Leicester Education Authority and returned to this after some time in the Royal Air Force during the war. From 1949 until 1956 he worked for the East Midlands Gas Board.

In his leisure time he wrote plays and often acted and assisted in amateur productions. In 1949 he eventually had his first play published. From then onwards several of his short plays were performed in amateur festivals and sometimes even given international prizes.

In 1956 he turned to drama full time, working as a television script-writer on a number of light comedy series. Two years later he joined the famous "Theatre-in-the Round" in Scarborough, a centre for talented writers and new ideas. David Campton stayed with that theatre group for six years and wrote a play for it each season.

Among his better-known plays are *The Laboratory* (1955), *Mutatis Mutandis* (1960) and *The Life and Death of Almost Everybody* (1970).

Incident was published in a collection of one-act plays in 1969. It deals with prejudice and belongs to the group of short plays in which Campton is particularly aware of his vision of people as helpless puppets trapped in frightening situations.

Unterrichtsvorschläge

Vorbemerkungen

1. Inhalt

In der Eingangshalle eines entlegenen und wenig belegten Dorfhotels nimmt die freundliche, junge, vom Land stammende Shirley Robinson in ihrer Funktion als Empfangsdame den Telefonhörer ab, um eine Buchung anzunehmen. Als sie jedoch vernimmt, daß am anderen Ende der Leitung ein gewisser Mr Smith spricht, schlägt die Stimmung sofort um. Shirley entschuldigt sich vielmals; das Hotel sei völlig ausgebucht, es gebe sicher weitere Hotels in der Umgebung, die möglicherweise noch freie Zimmer haben. Leicht verwirrt und mit Schuldgefühlen verläßt Shirley die Eingangshalle, um Miss Brown, die Managerin des Hauses, aufzusuchen.

Nach kurzer Zeit erreichen zwei Wanderinnen, Miss Jones und Miss Smith (!), das Hotel. Sie haben einen mühevollen Weg hinter sich und freuen sich auf eine gemütliche Unterkunft ('The promised land'; **16** 1). Vor allem Miss Smith, die durch Blasen an den Füßen stark beeinträchtigt ist, bedarf dringend der Ruhe und Stärkung. Intuitiv läßt sie sich deshalb gleich am offenen Feuer nieder. Beide Neuankömmlinge werden von der zurückkehrenden Shirley Robinson begrüßt. Mit den Formalitäten gibt es keine Probleme: Zwei Zimmer waren ja vorbestellt. Plötzlich jedoch – ein Blick auf die Unterschrift im Gästebuch offenbart es – bemerkt Shirley zu ihrem großen Entsetzen, daß eine der beiden Damen eine Smith ist. Sie gerät völlig außer Fassung, stürzt aus dem Raum und läßt die beiden leicht verwirrten Gäste zurück. Diese befinden sich inzwischen in Gesellschaft einer älteren Dame (Mrs Blake), die während Shirleys Eintragungsformalitäten aufkreuzte und beide, Miss Jones und Miss Smith, mit argwöhnisch stechendem Blick mustert. Alle Versuche, mit Mrs Blake ('a permanent resident') ins Gespräch zu kommen, scheitern an deren Unnahbarkeit.

Endlich tritt Miss Brown, die Hotel-Managerin, auf, gefolgt von Shirley. Sie ist eine aalglatte, stets lächelnde Dame. Sie versucht, die Angelegenheit als Mißverständnis darzustellen, bleibt jedoch hart in der Sache: Das Hotel sei besetzt und es gebe grundsätzlich keine Möglichkeit der Unterbringung – für jemand mit dem Namen Smith. Verstärkt wird die absurde Situation durch Mrs Blakes und Shirleys Horror-Darstellung: Anhand von vielen Beispielen verdeutlichen sie, daß alle Smiths böse und schuld an allem Übel im Land seien. Miss Jones und Miss Smith sind fassungslos. Miss Jones kämpft für ihre Freundin, die sich immer mehr zurückzieht und eigentlich gehen möchte. Schließlich wird ein Kompromiß gefunden: Miss Smith darf im Hotel-Anbau bleiben. Doch nun hat diese ihre Selbstachtung wiedergefunden. Sie verweigert die Annahme des Angebots. Es kommt zu einer heftigen Auseinandersetzung zwischen Miss Jones und Miss Smith, an deren Ende letztere das Hotel verläßt. Miss Jones Versuch, sie noch einzuholen, scheitert. Ohne ihre Freundin kehrt Miss Jones aus der nassen Dunkelheit zurück und hält den Hotel-Bewohnern den Spiegel vor. Mrs Blake wird bezichtigt, die eigene Existenz nur mit Feindbildern aufrechtzuhalten. Miss Brown wird als Opportunistin dargestellt, die ‚es eigentlich wissen müßte' und daher viel schlimmer als Mrs Blake sei (**34** 4–6). Dann verläßt auch Miss Jones den Ort. Zurück bleibt die unveränderte Welt des Hotels. Mrs Blake verbietet sich grundsätzlich eine nochmalige Störung dieser Art ('I was made to feel uncomfortable'; **34** 21), und Miss Brown betrachtet sich nach wie vor als diejenige, die das Heft fest in der Hand hat ('In complete control'; **34** 33).

Das Drama ist durch seine Symbolik vielfältig deutbar und dürfte trotz absurder Situation als *well-made short play* den Schülern leicht zugänglich sein.

2. Thematische Aspekte

Die in *Incident* angesprochenen Themenbereiche ermöglichen die Zuordnung des Werks zu verschiedenen Unterrichtsreihen. Als *parabel of our time* könnte das Drama eine Unterrichtsreihe über *England – a multiracial society* literarisch vervollständigen (*England* = Hotel, *the intruder* = Miss Smith). Das Werk kann darüber hinaus Inhalte literarisch abrunden, die das Problem des psychologischen und gesellschaftlichen Außenseiters, *prejudice* oder auch *education* zum Thema haben. Auch Themenstellungen und Begriffe wie Feindbild (Blake), Selbstachtung (Smith), Solidarität (Jones), Opportunismus (Brown) und Naivität (Shirley) werden im Drama dargestellt und können psychologische Unterrichtsreihen ergänzen. Nicht zuletzt bietet *Incident* die Möglichkeit der Exemplifizierung gattungsspezifischer Merkmale des *short play*.

3. Methodische Hinweise

Incident ist sprachlich relativ leicht zugänglich. Der Umfang des Werks legt jedoch eine schrittweise Aufteilung in *teaching units* nahe, die – wie im vorliegenden Fall – den dramatischen Ablauf des Geschehens widerspiegeln. Die *units* sind wiederum so angelegt, daß sie variabel handhabbar sind, d. h. die Lektüre kann durch die angebotenen Fragestellungen, Arbeitsaufträge, Hausaufgaben, Tafelbilder etc. und durch den Einsatz der Cassetten-Aufnahme abwechslungsreich gestaltet werden, wobei nicht nur das Verständnis des Werks abgesichert und vertieft werden soll, sondern auch Fragen erörtert werden können, die die angeschnittenen Themenbereiche inhaltlich nahelegen. Die Unterrichtselemente sind als Angebot zu verstehen, das sowohl eine intensive als auch eine extensive Behandlung des Dramas ermöglicht.

Der Einsatz der Cassette bedeutet einen kleinen Schritt in Richtung auf das *short play* als Bühnenkunstwerk. Ihr Einsatz im Unterricht (als Eröffnung oder Abschluß der Analyse) ist deshalb empfehlenswert.

4. *Incident* als Theaterstück

Das Werk ist für die Schulbühne sehr geeignet. Die fünf Frauenrollen sind nach Art und Umfang gleichwertig anzusetzen, und das Bühnenbild ist leicht zu gestalten. Die Handlung ist klar auf einen Höhepunkt hin angelegt, so daß auch Zuschauer mit weniger Englischkenntnissen folgen können. Erfahrungsgemäß bedeutet jede Art von Realisation auf der Bühne einen (auch emotional) besonders intensiven Zugriff zum Drama und zur englischen Sprache. Es sollte daher jede Möglichkeit der Darstellung wahrgenommen werden, weil die davon ausgehende positive Wirkung auf das sonstige Unterrichtsgeschehen nicht unerheblich sein dürfte.

Unit 1: The Telephone Call (**14** 1–**15** 22)

Der Einstieg in das Kurzdrama erfolgt am besten durch die gemeinsame Lektüre der *stage directions* und des Telefonats. Erfahrungsgemäß brauchen die Schüler etwas Zeit, um sich einzulesen. Beim anschließenden Vorspielen der Cassette sollten sie in der Lage sein, sich die Bühne vorzustellen und der Stimme Shirleys (mit leichtem Akzent) zu folgen.

1. *Draw a picture of the scenery according to the stage directions.*
Suggested drawing:

2. *Where does the description of the setting go beyond what can actually be shown on the stage (by the scenery)?*
The hotel is situated in a 'remote village, celebrated as a beauty spot'. Unless special posters or photos with fictitious names of the beauty spot or the hotel are used, the producer will find it rather difficult to express this detail on the actual stage.

3. *Which pieces of the scenery can be seen to convey 'communication'?*
- the two archways (= link between the world inside and outside)
- the two easy chairs and the settle (conversation)
- the counter with the telephone (technical link to the outside world)

4. *Imagine you are the producer of the play: What lighting and what sound effects would you suggest at the beginning?*

Lighting:
- spot on cubbyhole and telephone
- flickering fire (dimmed glow) reflected on settle and easy chairs
- possible change of light: cold-blue after Shirley has realized that it is a Smith who is calling

Sounds:
- cracking of fire
- wind blowing outside
- telephone ringing
- sudden hiss of rain

5. *Describe the development of the telephone call*
Shirley answers the phone. At first there are some difficulties with the connection. But after the connection has been established, Shirley is asked to reserve a room. She is just about to make the reservation when she is informed that the guest's name is Smith. There is an immediate (symbolic!) breakdown in the connection between her and the man at the other end of the line, as well as a complete change of mind. The phone seems to be 'out of focus'. Shirley pretends not to hear Mr Smith properly. After she realizes that she cannot go on blaming it solely on the phone, she apologizes and maintains that there isn't a single room left – although there are '20 rooms and 7 baths' (**15** 4). She tries to give reasons, suggests different hotels, and even warns Mr Smith not to come 'on spec' (**15** 12). All her attempts are aimed at emphasizing the fact that there won't be any room for this strange Mr Smith, not even in the hayloft. Shirley's behaviour and her sudden change of mind can be portrayed on the board in the following way (see overleaf), which also shows the development of the telephone call.

YES ⟶	change	⟶ NO	
A room?	S	Sometimes it gets out of focus.	blames it on the phone
I should think so.	M	But you see … The fact is … Strange as it may seem …	apologizes politely
Single or double?	I		
	T	There is no accommodation available.	refuses … … politely
	H	We haven't got a room. They are all full. There won't be any room for you. Not anywhere. Not even in the hayloft.	… categorically
		Half term hols. We fill up fast at the end of October.	gives reasons
	O	Don't you stop at this village at all. It's no use coming on spec.	gives a warning
		I'd drive straight on. The next village is …	suggests further possibilities

Homework:

1. *Describe Shirley's state of mind at the end of the telephone call.*
Shirley is unhappy because she feels that she has done something wrong. She is racked by feelings of guilt since she could have easily reserved a room for Mr Smith, who she even feels sorry for. ('You have got a car? … That's a blessing, isn't it, with the rain coming on …'; **15** 9–10). But on the other hand she obviously has to obey some strange regulations of the hotel. She is anxious about whether she acted properly and is torn between her conscience and some strange order. She troubles herself about whether her behaviour was appropriate or inconsiderate, because – after all – there might still be the possibility of Mr Smith suddenly turning up and checking. At last she calls Miss Brown (the manager) for help. Shirley's state of mind is symbolically underlined by the gusts of wind and rain outside.

2. *Complete the telephone conversation between Shirley and the mysterious Mr Smith by adding Mr Smith's part.*
The students could put in 'bits and pieces' as follows:

I can't hear straight.
I can't believe it.
It's really strange.
I'd be satisfied with any accommodation.
You're pulling my leg.
I'd even sleep in the hayloft.
No rooms at all? – impossible in autumn – out of season.
I'll just drop round and have a look and check.
Is there any other hotel nearby?
That simply can't be true.

Unit 2: The Arrival of the New Guests (**15** 23–**21** 6)

Durch eine gemeinsame (Vor-)Lektüre sollte das Textverständnis abgesichert werden, bevor die Cassette eingesetzt wird. Danach könnte das Unterrichtsgespräch durch folgende Fragen (bzw. Arbeitsaufträge) angeregt werden:

1. *According to the stage directions Miss Jones is described as 'a no-nonsense, capable person' (**15** 24) whereas Miss Smith is described as someone who 'seems more delicate – and considerate of other people' (**15** 25). Read lines **16** 1–**17** 20 and show whether the two characters behave (and speak) accordingly. Give examples.*

The students could cite the following examples:

	MISS JONES	MISS SMITH
Stage directions	'no-nonsense, capable person'	'seems more delicate – and considerate of other people'
Examples	● **She has a schedule.** – 'Behind schedule' (**16** 4) – 'panting to stride ahead' (**16** 11) ● **She accepts reality.** – 'Can't be helped. Blisters happen to the best of us.' (**16** 6) – 'We made it, didn't we?' (**16** 10) – 'We couldn't have gone any further.' (**16** 12–13)	● **She limps.** – sore heel, blisters ● **She apologizes/feels guilty** – 'Sorry.' (= It was my fault that we're behind schedule.) (**16** 5) – 'It's absurd, spoiling the outing for a sore heel.' (**16** 9) – 'I held you back.' (**16** 11)

Continued overleaf.

	MISS JONES	MISS SMITH
	● **She advises her friend.** – 'Take your weight off 'em.' (**16** 6) – 'Now relax.' (**16** 10/12) – 'You need a drink.' (**16** 16)	
	● **She turns to the counter.** – wants a room right away – looks for the bell (**16** 21) – raps on the counter (**16** 23) – shouts (**17** 1) – short matter-of-fact conversation with Shirley	● **She turns to the fire.** ● **She wants a bed and a bath.** ● **She is tired.** – she almost falls asleep

2. *What sort of clothing should the two friends wear?*
Suggestions:
Miss Jones: a waterproof jacket, blue jeans, rubber boots, etc.
Miss Smith: glasses, a blue anorak, tennis or track shoes, corduroy trousers, a headscarf, etc.

3. *What information about the hotel does Shirley give the newcomers on p. **17**, l. 21–31 and why does this arouse the curiosity of the audience? (Refer also to Shirley's telephone call at the beginning.)*
The audience shares with Shirley knowledge of which Miss Jones and Miss Smith are ignorant: they know that Shirley told a lie when she informed a certain Mr Smith of the fact that the hotel was fully booked up, since they now get the information that there are only two other guests and that there is 'space for another twenty – not counting the annexe' (**17** 21–22). They are also informed that the hotel even provides special rates for permanent guests out of season, and that there is 'one permanent for the time being' (**17** 27–28). Expectations are aroused in the audience or reader about the future course of events, because although Shirley is being very amiable, she might suddenly change her mind, as during the telephone call.

4. *Shirley suddenly realizes that Miss Jones' companion is called Miss Smith (**18** 25–27). How does she behave before and after this realization?*
Before Shirley realizes that the limping lady is a Smith she behaves normally: she is communicative and ready to talk and give a lot of information about the hotel and its guests. When she sees that Miss Smith has 'damaged' herself (**18** 15), she shows sympathy and offers to help. After her discovery

she is not only surprised, but also shocked. (*'Her smile fades ... she stares at* MISS SMITH.'; **18** 26–27). She feels awkward, stops carrying Miss Smith's pack, feels guilty and at a loss. She tries to find arguments to prove her innocence and 'scurries out'. The change of her state of mind has a striking resemblance to the one in the first scene (during the telephone conversation).

Suggestions for the blackboard:

SHIRLEY'S REALIZATION

BEFORE ——————————————————→ AFTER

Shirley

- **is communicative**
  tells the guests that there is enough space in the hotel
- **shows sympathy**
  'Have you damaged yourself?' (**18** 15)
  'Blister! They're wicked things.' (**18** 17)
  'Poor lamb! No wonder you're worn out.' (**18** 22)
- **is helpful**
  offers to look for a bandage (**18** 18)
  carries Miss Smith's pack (**18** 24)

S M I T H !

Shirley

- **is shocked**
  smile fades (**18** 26)
  stares at Miss Smith (**18** 27)
  feels awkward
- **defends herself**
  'You didn't say.'
  (**18** 31, **19** 1, **19** 11)
  'How was I to know?' (**19** 4)
  'I can't tell by just looking.' (**19** 4)
  'She can't blame me' (**19** 10)
  'I wasn't told.' (**19** 10)
- **stops helping Miss Smith**
  puts down the pack (**18** 26)
- **is helpless and must look for help**
  'What am I to do now?' (**19** 4–5)
  'I'm not sure that ...' (**19** 7)
- **scurries out**

5. *Describe Mrs Blake and people's reaction to her.*
Mrs Blake is 'an elderly lady' (probably wearing a tweed suit) 'with a piercing eye' (**17** 31–32). 'The intensity of her gaze' (**19** 25) seems to be a dominant element of her character. She 'studies the group at the desk' (**17** 32–33), stares at Shirley, Miss Jones and Miss Smith (**19** 24) and her 'close scrutiny' (**20** 1) makes everybody feel uncomfortable. Shirley stops talking when she appears and then utters a hoarse whisper (**18** 4) as if she were afraid of her.

Mrs Blake shuns contact with other people. She rebukes Shirley for trying to introduce her to the newcomers (**18** 5–6). When Miss Jones and Miss

Smith try to begin a conversation, she doesn't answer (**20** 1). She refuses to speak at all (**20** 4) or sits in an attitude which clearly suggests that she isn't listening (**20** 17). She seems to be deaf, because all attempts at establishing some kind of communication prove futile. Miss Smith falters and gives up (**21** 1–2); Miss Jones is becoming more and more irritated and is on the point of losing her temper (**20** 3/19/27, **21** 6). Notice the series of prolonged pauses (**20** 1/2/3/8/18/29, **21** 1/2), which work powerfully in that they create a contrasting tension and intensify the atmosphere of general awkwardness and embarrassment.

6. *'I am deaf in one ear. I am blind in one eye!' (**21** 3)*
*'I see what I want to see, I hear what I want to hear.' (**21** 5)*
Comment on these lines.
Mrs Blake seems to be deaf, but apparently her hearing is not defective at all. She is able even to hear Shirley's whisper (**18** 4). Her sight also seems to be quite selective. At first she studies the strangers with a piercing eye, then she turns away from them and ignores them. But she is well aware of what is going on. When Shirley is shocked by the discovery of the name 'Smith' in the register, Mrs Blake asks 'Another?' (= Another Smith?; **18** 28).

7. *Describe the theatrical function of Shirley's and Mrs Blake's behaviour.*
The newly arrived guests are puzzled and embarrassed by Shirley's and Mrs Blake's behaviour. Although Miss Jones seems to be in control of the situation, she wonders whether something might be wrong with Shirley (**20** 23). In addition to this, she definitely finds it difficult to understand Mrs Blake. She and Miss Smith are both bewildered by the fact that everybody and everything turns out to be strange, hostile and cold. Intuitively Miss Smith crouches by the fire and Miss Jones stands 'firmly in front of the fire, 'as though defying anyone to move her' (**19** 26–27). The theatrical suspense arises from the fact that the audience by now suspect that the strange situation is caused by Miss Smith being a 'Smith', whereas the two characters on the stage haven't been able to link the situation up with the name (*dramatic irony*).

8. *What does Miss Smith have in mind when she says: 'After all, we are in England?' (**21** 1)*
The situation in the hotel has turned rather mysterious and unsettling. Miss Smith feels it important to reassure herself that everything will turn out all right, that she is basically safe, because she is in England – the epitome of law and order –, where people behave sensibly. Of course, this will prove to be a rather ironical statement.

Homework:
*The text contains a number of references to the **rain**, the **snow**, the **fire** and the **hotel furniture**. How do they reflect the course of the action?*

RAIN: *Refer to **15** 10, **15** 22, **16** 3, **17** 15, **19** 28, **20** 2–6.*
The rain presents a sharp contrast to the sheltered security of the hotel. Miss Jones and Miss Smith have only just missed this rain, which might stand for the 'nasty' world outside in comparison to the hotel, which is hailed as 'the promised land' (**16** 1). When Mrs Blake refuses to reply and Miss Jones gradually becomes irritated, the latter cites the weather forecast: 'A shallow depression' ... 'Storms are expected in all areas. Temperatures will be sub-normal, with frost on high ground' (**20** 4–6). These lines reflect the cold atmosphere in the hotel and the fact that the 'climate' there has turned unpleasant.

FIRE: *Refer to **16** 14, **19** 18, **19** 26.*
Miss Smith is attracted by the warmth of the fire, which is real – in contrast to the 'phoney' furnishing and decor. The fire might be the symbol of hope and shelter. Significantly, the fire place is situated in the centre of the front stage (although it is 'assumed' to be there – not actually to be seen by the audience).

HOTEL DECOR: *Refer to **16** 1, **16** 14, **19** 15–16, **19** 19–20.*
The furniture and the interior design of the entrance hall of the hotel are old-fashioned ('Olde Englishe knick-knacks'; **16** 1). Whereas 'no-nonsense' Miss Jones comments on it ironically, Miss Smith distrusts the place ('The brassware may be **fake**'; **16** 14; '**cardboard** panelling and **phoney** beams'; **19** 15–16) and finally realizes that the hotel is simply cold, 'for all the Olde Englishe trappings' (**19** 19–20), i. e. in spite of the outward signs of wealth, comfort and prestige. For her the hotel is certainly not 'the promised land'.

SNOW: *Refer to **16** 24–27.*
Miss Smith's line 'never go to sleep in the snow' anticipates the unpleasant turn of events. 'Snow' could stand for the hotel, which turns out to be a cold, hostile place. She feels she shouldn't trust it – she should stay awake.

Unit 3: 'A Smith is a Smith' (**21** 7–**27** 12)

Die relative Dichte der Argumentationen der verschiedenen Charaktere legt für diesen Teil eine vorentlastende Lektüre des Texts nahe. Danach kann die Cassette gehört werden. Die durch die folgenden Fragen gelenkte Analyse bezieht sich zunächst auf den Inhalt. Eine abschließende Wertung und Deutung der in den jeweiligen Aussagen implizierten Haltungen und Konzepte erfolgt sinnvollerweise erst am Ende der Lektüre (außer Frage 7).

1. *How does Miss Brown cope with the situation?*
Miss Brown, the manager, is 'in full control' (**22** 14). She plays her role perfectly. Her permanent smile is simply a means of concealing her hard-

ness. Apparently she has 'risen in the world' from a lower social class, and is at pains to hide her 'common' accent and background. (Cf. **21** 7–8: '*She speaks correctly, but rather like someone who has learned to speak that way.*')

She readily accepts all responsibility (**22** 14) and apologizes (**21** 18), though indirectly reproaching Miss Jones ('You made no mention of a Miss Smith'; **21** 20–21). On the other hand she remains firm and refuses categorically to offer Miss Smith any room at all. The situation has become absurd; but what crowns it all is that Miss Brown simply tells a lie when she maintains that the hotel is full (**22** 7). Ironically enough she deliberately avoids the word 'refusal' (**22** 17) to save her (smiling) face and to keep up the hotel's principle of having 'a reputation for hospitality' (**21** 31). Obviously not only the decor, but also the management of the hotel is 'phoney'.

2. *What sort of clothing should Miss Brown wear?*
Miss Brown is the essence of efficiency, possibly wearing a red-coloured suit, bobbed hair, golden rings, fashionable shoes; face perfectly made up; dressed rather formally.

3. *Miss Smith and Mrs Blake suddenly change places (**22** 20–25). What is the theatrical function of this action?*
Miss Smith is sitting on the settle and Mrs Blake on a chair by the coffee table. When Miss Smith goes to and sits on the other chair by the coffee table, Mrs Blake gets up (possibly abruptly) and goes over to the settle to indicate her hatred of Miss Smith. The audience's attention is deliberately drawn to her, because she is the person who takes on the responsibility of explaining to the visitors exactly what the cause of the trouble is – whereas Miss Brown seems too embarrassed to broach the subject. It is Mrs Blake who is the first to 'call a spade a spade'. (Refer also to **25** 6 and **26** 6, where Mrs Blake shrinks from Miss Smith.)

4. *What does Mrs Blake think of all Smiths?*
According to Mrs Blake the Smiths are the embodiment of wickedness, the incarnation and root of evil and 'a menace to the English way of life' (**24** 25). Together they make a powerful force, and make up a race apart. They are a stigmatized set of people, who are arrogant, powerful, rich (with doubtful sources of income; **26** 28–**27** 2) and who outnumber the rest (**24** 2–4). They cling together, they worry people (**24** 5), they are a 'disease' (**24** 13), they 'smell' (**26** 8) and even the mere pronunciation of the word 'Smith' causes an inner struggle and is obviously distasteful (**21** 17, **23** 7–8, **23** 17). They are to be found everywhere: 'They crawl through our daily life' (**24** 12–13) and can be found in every area of public life (**24** 16–19) and commerce (**24** 22–23; this is a very amusing reference to genuine British firms: W. H. Smiths are nationwide booksellers). Mrs Blake speaks bluntly about the Smiths. She doesn't regard it as a personal matter, let alone a personal

insult ('Not that I hold anything against the young woman personally'; **22** 26–27; 'I've no wish to hurt anyone'; **22** 34). But on the other hand she blames her own fate on the Smiths. She makes out that they have profoundly affected her life as an old age pensioner (**25** 17–**26** 4, **27** 1–2), especially economically. She blames the Smith 'clan' for inflation, which has eaten up her savings. Therefore she focusses all her hatred, disgust, contempt and envy on them.

5. *Describe the character of Mrs Blake according to what she says about the Smiths.*
Mrs Blake is an elderly lady, who holds old-fashioned and conservative views. She thinks, for example, that girls should be nice and sweet, devoted to their parents and fond of animals (**22** 27–28) – which implies a satire on 'olde Englishe' attitudes. She is also the mouthpiece of all frustrated and prejudiced people, who find fault with everything and who, psychologically speaking, can only establish their own identity by believing that there is some enemy that has to be fought against. Therefore she appears to be stubborn, unyielding, wooden and uncompromising. Ironically, she behaves just like the Smiths she describes and who she feels so endangered and molested by.

6. *What does Shirley Robinson think about the Smiths?*
Personally she would not reject them. She always stresses the fact that she 'was told' that they were nasty (**23** 31, **24** 8/14/20/24/27). British education is revealed in a ridiculous light through her views. To her, the name Smith is 'not nice' (**23** 31), the Smiths are different (**24** 9), false and cruel (**24** 20–21), and 'ought never to have been let into the country' (**24** 27). Funnily enough they 'never use handkerchiefs' (**24** 24) and are used as 'bogeymen' to frighten children into behaving well (**24** 14–15). The fact that she is eventually cut short by Miss Brown, the manager, ('That will do, Miss Robinson'; **24** 29) shows that she is (ab)used as a political mouthpiece, who is to back up Miss Brown ... but not allowed to go too far.

The answers to questions 4–6 can be summarized on the board in the following way (see overleaf):

MISS BLAKE	SHIRLEY
Hatred, disgust, contempt	… was told (education and upbringing at home)
SMITH	
● **a special set of people a stigmatized class** 'A Smith is a Smith.' (**23** 20) 'It runs in the blood.' (**23** 20) a 'tribe' (**23** 23)	● **different** not 'our sort' (**24** 9)
● **negative aspects** powerful (**24** 6) wealthy, doubtful sources of income (**26** 28–**27** 2) dangerous; outnumber the rest (**24** 4) they smell (**26** 8/11) they are a disease (**24** 13)	● **negative aspects** the name is 'not nice' (**23** 31) they do you down (**24** 20) they never use a handkerchief (**24** 24)
● **they are eveywhere** 'They crawl through our daily life' (**24** 12–13), can be found in law, medicine, politics, church, army, navy, air force, police, prison, Commons, Lords, BBC, commerce, etc.	● **something ought to be done about them** 'They ought never to have been let in the country in the first place!' (**24** 27–28)
● **responsible for Mrs Blake's fate** (**25** 17–**26** 4)	● **Smiths = bogeymen** (**24** 24)
Smith = the embodiment of wickedness and evil; 'a menace to the English way of life' (**24** 25)	**Smith** = nasty people

7. *What kind of people could the Smiths stand for?*
Some of the information given about them might indicate that they could stand for ethnic groups, any foreigners or people from abroad (they smell; **26** 8/11); 'They ought never to have been let in the country' (**24** 27). In this respect the absurd cluster of negative aspects associated with the Smiths could be a criticism of the insane and even traumatic fear of a new multicultural society in England, which seems to be a vital question to all 'Blakes'. It would also account for prejudice still being an important aspect of school and home life according to what Shirley says. Thus the exaggerated description of the 'Smiths' can be regarded as a satire on the concept of prejudice. Of course, a parallel could also be seen here with the prejudice against the Irish, Scots, Welsh, Jews, etc. Moreover, since they penetrate all areas of commercial, public, political, religious and administrative life, the Smiths could also represent any irresponsible, egoistic, reckless and 'nasty' group in English society.

Homework:
The situation has become absurd. Describe Miss Jones' and Miss Smith' reaction to it. (Before answering this question, read the text again closely: ***21*** *7–**27** 12).*
Miss Jones is unwilling to accept the rejection of Miss Smith. She is a 'no-nonsense' type of character who at first dismisses the trouble as a clerical error and as a ridiculous case of 'red tape'. In addition, she ironically points out the contradiction between Miss Brown's and Shirley's statements about the availability of accommodation. But soon she realizes that she cannot achieve anything by force of argument. She is completely thrown off balance and absolutely nonplussed by the strange behaviour of the people at the hotel ('Where's the logic?'; **22** 35). She senses that everything is beyond her grasp now and she can therefore only react emotionally. She turns aggressive and is ready to fight for her friend's rights (**27** 11). It's now a matter of self-respect and for this reason she tries to force her friend to stay.

Miss Smith on the other hand is more considerate of 'poor' Mrs Blake (**26** 5) and of Shirley. She would be satisfied with any room (**22** 1) – at least at first. She even tries to get into contact with Mrs Blake by moving over to her and stretching her hand out (**22** 21–25, **25** 6, **26** 6). But since she is a delicate and vulnerable person, she is soon completely bewildered by the absurd situation she finds herself in. In the end she cannot bear it any longer. When Mrs Blake says that she 'smells' (**26** 8/11) she recoils with a cry and is ready to leave (**26** 15). She realizes that what they believe is absurd, but she also realizes the dreadful implications of the fact **that** they believe it (**26** 23).

Suggestions for a summary on the board:

Miss Jones ➡ **SMITH** = not allowed in the hotel ⬅ Miss Smith

Miss Jones

- **is unwilling to accept the rejection**
  - 'piece of red tape' (**21** 24)
  - 'Nonsense' (**21** 34); 'talk sense' (**22** 4)
  - points out contradiction: Miss Brown says: no rooms, Shirley said: lots of rooms (**22** 7–9)
- **can't grasp the absurdity of the situation**
  - 'Will someone translate?' (**22** 29)
  - 'Where's the logic?' (**22** 35)
  - 'A what?' (**23** 9)
  - 'I'm losing my grip on reality. You're not real ... delirium ... fever ...' (**23** 12–15)
- **feels ashamed of being a teacher**
  feels responsible for Shirley's education (**25** 1–3)
- **feels provoked**
  - calls Miss Brown a liar (**23** 4)
  - almost loses self-control (**23** 6)
  - doesn't want her friend to give in (**26** 18)
  - is ready to fight (**27** 11)
- **forces her friend to STAY**

Miss Smith

- **is friendly**
  - would be satisfied with any other room (**22** 1)
  - tries to establish some contact with Mrs Blake, stretches hand out (**22** 21–25, **25** 6, **26** 6)
- **can't grasp the absurdity of the situation**
  - 'I don't believe it.' (**22** 20)
  - 'Suddenly I'm untouchable?' (**22** 32)
  - 'My name? Because of my name ...' (**23** 11)
  - But my name's only a word' (**23** 16)
  - 'You're afraid – of me?' (**24** 7)
  - 'We're human. ...' (**25** 12–13)
- **is hurt**
  - 'Stop it!' (**24** 26)
  - 'recoils with a cry' (**26** 9)
  - struggles 'to keep her composure' (**26** 12)
- **wants to GO, but is forced to stay**

Unit 4: The Compromise and Miss Smith's Refusal
(**27** 13–**32** 15)

Wieder empfiehlt sich die Lektüre dieses Abschnitts vor dem Anhören der Cassette.

1. *How is a compromise reached between Miss Brown and Miss Jones? (**27** 13–**29** 13)*
Miss Jones is ready to fight. So is Miss Brown, who readily takes up the gauntlet in order to safeguard the reputation of her premises. After all, she has worked for it: some time ago the place was considered 'a den of iniquity' (**27** 20–21), but after she took over, it was soon turned into what it is now. She regards it as her duty to keep up high standards even though this 'may call for the occasional sacrifice' (**27** 13). Molly Jones tries to attack this weak point. By hinting at Miss Smith's pitiable state ('she is lame'; **28** 10) and by picturing her spending a wet night under a hedge or even collapsing altogether somewhere in the bad weather (**28** 16–17), she accuses Miss Brown of ruthlessness. In addition to this she warns her of possible consequences ('I won't let you all forget this evening in a hurry'; **28** 22). At last Miss Brown gives in and suggests the possibility of the annexe. Although she regards it as 'a useful second best' (**29** 5), which – incidentally – will not include use of the dining-room, she considers it a satisfactory solution (**29** 13). Miss Jones, however, regards it only as a compromise.

2. *What is the theatrical function of this scene?*
So far, the situation has become more and more critical. But now a solution seems to have been reached, and there is a certain relaxation of suspense.

3. *How does Miss Smith react?*
At the beginning of this section Miss Smith gives up her self-respect by accepting Mrs Brown's refusal. ('I don't think Smiths are allowed self-respect. They either crawl away, or sit back ...'; **27** 31–**28** 2). She is desperate and depressed and wants to go. But while others fight over her rights, she gradually regains her self-respect. Eventually she is able to make her own decisions and refuse the compromise. Her friend Miss Jones is taken aback, and the audience is interested in how she will cope with the new situation.

Suggestions for summing up questions 1–3 on the board are made on p 76.

4. *Describe the personal disagreement between Miss Jones and Miss Smith about Miss Smith's refusal to accept the compromise (**29** 24–**32** 24).*
Miss Jones is surprised to see that her friend doesn't accept the offer. After all, she has fought for her. Now she is shocked and disappointed ('Are you

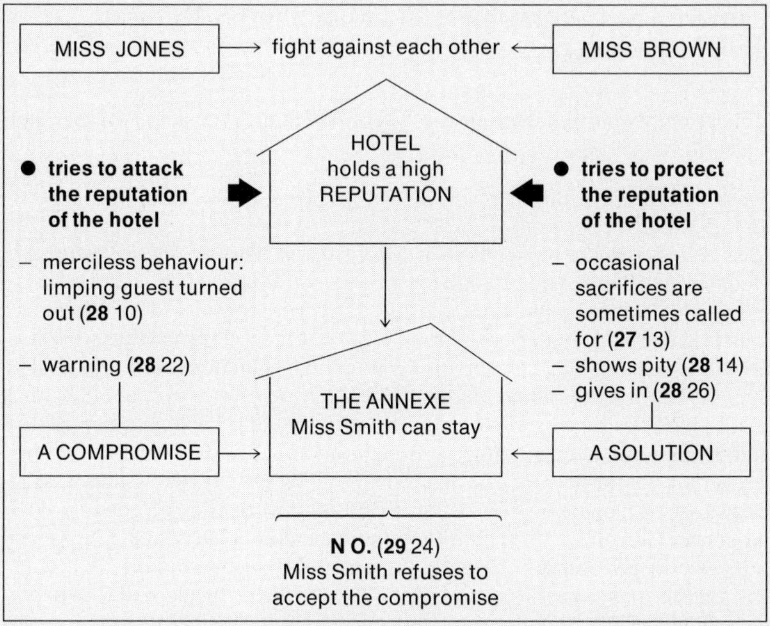

Blackboard suggestions for questions 1–3 on p 75.

telling me I might have saved my breath?'; **31** 5). Her friend has dealt her a severe blow. Miss Smith on the other hand has regained her self-respect (**31** 10). She appreciates everybody's commitment to agree on a compromise ('It was a kind gesture'; **30** 3–5), but has 'no intention of accepting the second-class label' (**30** 13). She would feel discriminated against ('it's the division ... Sheep from goat'; **30** 7). Now she has decided to behave and think independently, without feeling ashamed of herself any longer. She picks up her pack and leaves. Her friend Molly is stunned. She recovers, however, quite quickly and tries to persuade Miss Smith to stay. She puts forward sound arguments ('It's still raining'; **30** 22), refers to her efforts ('I did my best'; **31** 25), feels offended and held up to ridicule ('Are you leaving me to their sniggers?'; **32** 1), warns her friend of the consequences of her refusal (**31** 7–9), gets angry and accuses her of stubbornness and unreasonableness (**31** 14/17). But all her endeavours prove futile. At last she loses her temper altogether, calls Miss Smith a fool (**32** 15) and washes her hands of the whole affair, only to regret her outburst almost immediately.

5. *What is the function of the disagreement between the two friends?*
Certainly the relationship between the two women has come to a serious crisis closely connected with an identity crisis. Psychologically speaking, Molly Jones collapses. It takes a little while for her outburst to pass. Then she regains her feeling of solidarity. She dashes out through the right archway and follows her friend Dora.

The function of this scene is to prepare for a change of action. Again suspense is created.

Questions 4–5 could be summed up on the board like this:

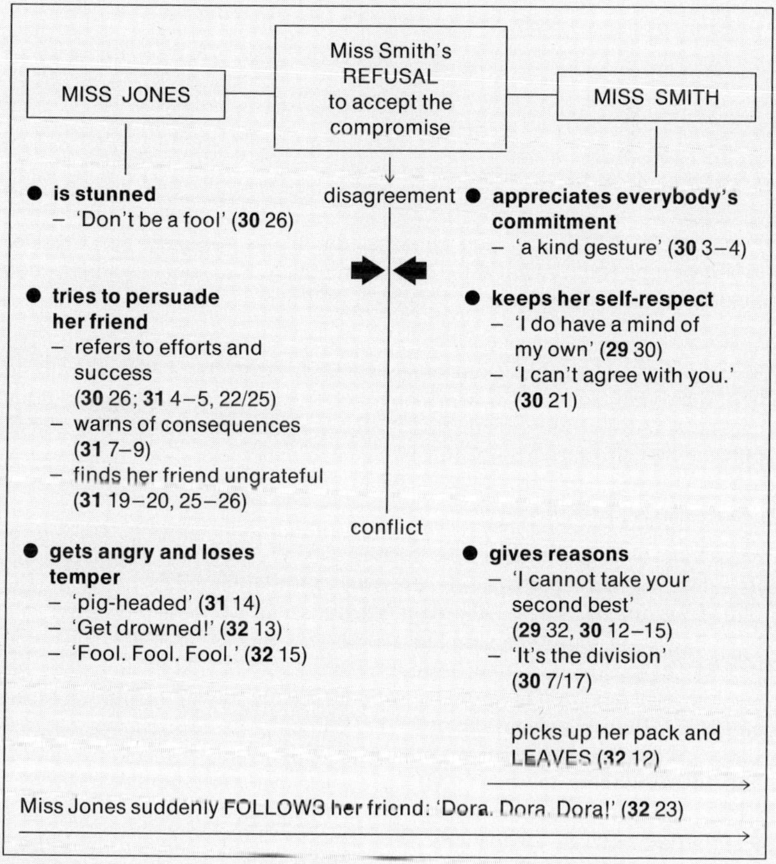

Homework:
*What is the function of the short interlude after Miss Smith's and Miss Jones' departure (**32** 25–35)?*
Shirley suggests the old boathouse (for accommodating Miss Smith) and both characters, Shirley as well as the manager, feel sorry for all Smiths ('Smith. It's a pity'; **32** 29). The little interlude separates Miss Smith's and Miss Jones' departure from Miss Jones' return. It is a theatrical device to make the time between Miss Jones' departure and her return more plausible.

Unit 5: Miss Jones' Return (**33** 1–**34** 33)

Das Ende des Dramas kann zunächst durch das Anhören der Cassette erfaßt werden (mit Fragen zum Grobverständnis). Nach der anschließenden Lektüre können die folgenden Fragen gestellt werden.

1. *What happens to Miss Smith?*
Miss Smith has vanished ('out of sight'; **33** 3). Miss Jones returns without her. She doesn't even know which direction she took. Her description of the darkness and the rain outside and Shirley's remark about the river (**33** 7) indicate the hardships Miss Smith will have to undergo and the danger she is in.

2. *How does Miss Jones feel when she returns and how does she react?*
Miss Jones is sad, subdued and worried. She feels depressed because her friend has left her – perhaps forever – and, considering the darkness and the rain, fears for her safety. She feels ashamed and wonders how she could have ended on the other side (**33** 19, **34** 8), i. e. how and why she could possibly have agreed that her friend 'wasn't one of us' (**34** 8). She feels she has betrayed her friend – and her own ideals ('I let down the human race'; **34** 16–17). Before leaving, she utters her contempt for Miss Brown and Mrs Blake. She accuses Miss Brown of being an opportunist ('You know better, but still you join in the hunt'; **34** 1–2; 'You crawl'; **34** 5) and despises Mrs Blake, the 'poor, scared, old lady' (**33** 22), who needs 'villains' (**33** 29–32) in order to survive. In the end Miss Jones follows Miss Smith, though realizing that it is only 'a futile gesture' (**34** 15). She wants to make up for what has happened.

Suggestions for the blackboard:

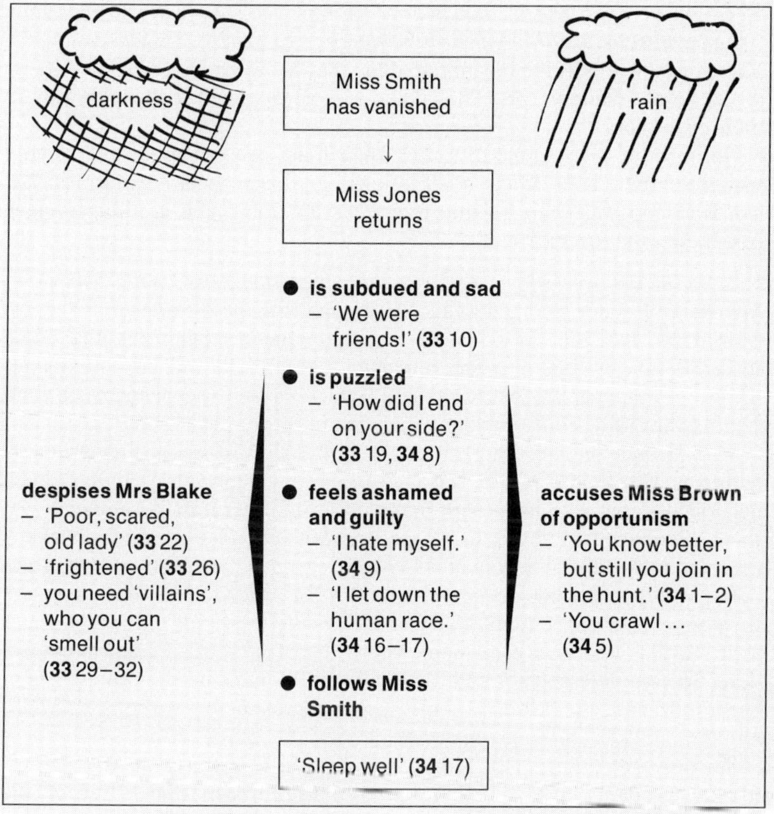

3. *What is the meaning of Miss Jones' line 'There'll always be somebody under the axe' (34 11)?*

Miss Jones wants to point out that it seems to be a common feature of the human race, even a matter of identity for many people – represented by Mrs Blake – to blame some 'villain' (**33** 29) for all nasty things 'waiting round the corner' (**33** 26). And since the latter will always be the case, the Blakes in this world will constantly be trying to gain confidence and the hope of security by 'smelling out' (**33** 29) people who are not like them and who they therefore must get rid of. Miss Jones' enumeration in **33** 30–31 ('people with funny-shaped noses …') is to point out how arbitrary and absurd their criteria are, and in **34** 12–13 she indicates that each of the persons present might one day belong to the group of outcasts: Cockneys = Miss Brown, schoolteachers = herself, ladies over sixty = Mrs Blake.

4. *Compare Miss Jones' final words ('Sleep well'; **34** 17) with her line: 'Wonder if we're disturbing their hibernation' (**16** 18–19).*
Miss Jones' words at the beginning of the play are symbolic: The inhabitants of the hotel – Shirley, Miss Brown and Mrs Blake – will stick stubbornly to their prejudices.

No intruder will be able to disturb their long, deep sleep during the cold winter of their lives (their hibernation). In this respect Miss Jones' last words 'Sleep well' can be interpreted as an ironic and scathing remark concluding the drama.

5. *Describe the psychological state of the others after Miss Jones' departure.*
Mrs Blake has not changed at all. She is glad that the intruders have disappeared and that life can resume its normal course. ('Dinner is now being served, I take it?'; **32** 35). She remains a 'permanent' indeed. She blames the hotel manager for her weakness, which caused the disturbance, and reminds her of her duty to take a firm line in future (**34** 19–23).

Miss Brown on the other hand seems deeply disturbed. She probably feels that Miss Jones' reproach was justified, but she is not prepared to risk her social status. She hates Mrs Blake because of her unfair comments; yet she feels obliged to bottle up her anger. Her dependence on Mrs Blake is revealed in the amusing way in which she 'corrects' herself from 'Oh, go to hell' (**34** 24) to 'I said – very well' (**34** 26). In order to vent her anger she then hisses a sarcastic remark at Shirley. Finally she holds onto the register as if seeking assurance from somewhere. Her last words ('I am in control here. In complete control'; **34** 31–32) ironically indicate the hollowness of her life. In fact, she herself is controlled by forces she has no control over at all.

We only get one hint of Shirley's emotions: She stares at Miss Brown (**34** 28), probably puzzled by her muttered insult to Mrs Blake. Earlier, she showed some real concern for Miss Smith (cf. **32** 26, **33** 7), but she will probably soon have forgotten the incident and is glad when Miss Brown sends her away.

Unit 6: Further Structural and Thematic Aspects of the Play

1. *Describe the various characters of the play, their relation to one another, and say what they might represent.*
Mrs Blake, 'an elderly lady with a piercing eye' (**17** 31–32), who sees what she wants to see and hears what she wants to hear (**21** 5), focusses all her

hatred, her disgust and her contempt on Miss Smith. Although she has nothing against Miss Smith personally, she regards herself as a victim of all Smiths. They are everywhere and responsible for her deplorable economic situation.

Mrs Blake, the 'permanent resident for the time being' (**17** 27), might represent conservativism in England. She also stands for people who always try to find 'villains' or people 'not like us' (**33** 30), who can be blamed for the nasty things 'waiting round the corner' (**33** 26).

Miss Brown, who was brought up in the slums of East London has made a social and economic career. She wears an almost permanent smile and carefully hides her Cockney accent (cf. **21** 7–9). She would do anything to maintain her status, even to the extent of doing an injustice to other people or giving up her self-respect. She is dependent on Mrs Blake. She 'crawls' to people like her (**34** 4–5) in order to keep up the reputation of the hotel. Miss Brown might represent the recklessness and egoism of businessmen/ women, officialdom in general or the (smiling) hollowness and insincerity of (British?) politicians.

Shirley Robinson, the friendly young country girl is inwardly torn between her sympathy for Miss Smith and her compulsion, caused by her upbringing, to shun all Smiths because they are 'not nice' and don't use handkerchiefs. She might represent the mass of uncritical people who need to conform to public opinion and who are easily indoctrinated.

Miss Molly Jones is 'a no-nonsense, capable person'. She helps and fights for her friend Miss Smith. She takes a firm stand, but finally agrees on a compromise. When she is denied gratitude for her efforts – Miss Smith refuses to accept the compromise –, she reacts aggressively. She soon finds out that her friendship is based on pity. Only when she follows her friend in the dark and rain is she true to herself. Before leaving she reveals the truth to the inhabitants of the hotel.

Miss Molly Jones might represent common sense, critical intelligence, nonconformism as well as the political opposition or – psychologically speaking – the guilty conscience of the nation.

Miss Dora Smith is a delicate person and considerate of other people. She longs to stay in the hotel, but is denied accommodation. She can hardly believe what is happening. She feels offended, insulted, and is not only the object of Mrs Blake's hatred, but also of Miss Jones' and Miss Brown's negotiations. After having regained her self-respect she can no longer endure the absurdity of the grotesque situation. This is why she even decides to leave her friend.

In the drama she is the outcast, the untouchable, the scapegoat, the embodiment of (imaginary!) evil, but she also represents the concept of self-respect.

Suggestions for the blackboard (see overleaf):

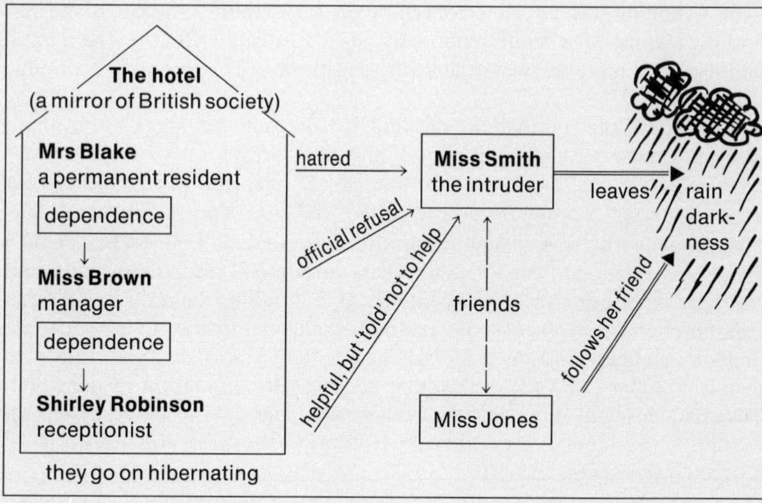

NB: The term 'permanent resident' is very commonly used in GB – there are a lot of elderly people staying at hotels as permanent residents.

2. *Describe the structure of the plot.*
The interaction of the various characters gradually builds up tension until a turning-point is reached and the tension is released. This may be shown in the following diagram:

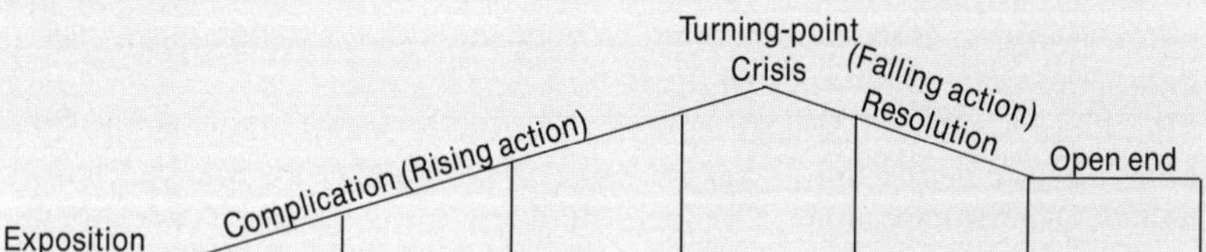

Description of the scene; Shirley's telephone call	Arrival of Miss Jones and Miss Smith	The reaction of Shirley, Mrs Blake, Miss Brown to 'a Smith'	The fight and the compromise	Miss Smith's refusal and departure	Miss Jones teaches inhabitants a lesson and leaves	Miss Brown 'in complete control'
14 1–**15** 22	**15** 23–**18** 25	**18** 26–**26** 13	**26** 14–**29** 23	**29** 24–**32** 35	**33** 1–**34** 18	**34** 19–33

3. *What could be the symbolic meaning of the 'hotel'?*
Suggested answers:
- The hotel might represent Britain/British society/society in general.
- The hotel is the 'promised land', the place of hope and warmth (fireplace), where not only Mrs Blake is accepted as a permanent resident, but where Miss Smith expects and hopes for shelter (drink, bed, etc.).
- The hotel is also a cold place with phoney furniture (representing general insincerity), where some guests (like the Smiths) are regarded as intruders, even if they have blisters and take refuge from the darkness and the rain. For all the 'Olde Englishe trappings' (**19** 19) it isn't such a friendly place. Appearances can be deceptive.
- The hotel is a grotesque, nightmarish, fantastic place where life – or people's attitude to it – seems strangely distorted.
- The hotel is a place whose inhabitants 'hibernate', i. e. where they are not fully aware of reality and where they live in their own world of prejudice, shut off from others of a different type from themselves.
  (For the symbolic meaning of the '**rain/fire/hotel decor/snow**' see p 69.)

4. *What could the title mean*
The word 'incident' has two basic meanings:
1. It is used for an event or happening of minor importance.
2. It is also used for a disturbance, often connected with violence.

The title is deliberately ambiguous. It is up to the audience to interpret it – or to change their interpretation in the course of the play.

5. *What might be the message of the play?*
Suggested answers:
- *Incident* is a play that holds up a mirror to the audience by depicting the absurdity of prejudice.
  (A point worth mentioning is the ironical choice of names for the charac ters: 'Smith' is a very common name and so are 'Jones', 'Brown' and 'Robinson'. This indicates the complete arbitrariness of prejudice – if 'Smith', why not 'Jones' or 'Brown'?)
- *Incident* is committed to the idea of a pluralistic, multicultural society in Britain. It is a criticism of the notion that England is a tolerant, wonderful beauty spot.
- *Incident* is a psychological play. The audience (reader) is forced into the internal logic of the drama and is confronted with the absurd rejection of anyone called Smith, which is funny on the surface, and yet soon arouses feelings of fear and indignation
- *Incident* is a psychological 'morality' play on **naivety** and **conformism** (Shirley), **prejudice** and **intolerance** (Blake), **opportunism** (Brown), **solidarity** (Jones) and **self-respect** (Smith).

For further discussion

1. Discuss the open end of the drama.
2. There are 5 female characters in the play. Why?
3. Comment on the time structure of the play: late evening, late autumn (end of October).
4. Would you call *Incident* an absurd drama?
5. Do you feel sorry for Miss Smith? Would you act in the same way as her friend Miss Jones?
6. Would you say that *Incident* is a parable of our time?

Lyndon Brook

Score

Characters:

HARRY

SHEILA

Scene:

A tennis net is stretched across stage over the floats. HARRY *and* SHEILA, *in white, hold rackets, but mime the use of tennis balls.*

HARRY *(not pleased)*: That's another game to you two ... *(Lifts his head at some remark from our side of the net.)* Now Jim! Don't you start feeling sorry for us – this is all part of our tactics, we're lulling you into a false sense of superiority!

SHEILA *(collecting balls upstage)*: False?

HARRY *(to query from* JANE*)*: Score? Ah yes ... *(Clicking his fingers at* SHEILA*)* Sheila, what's the score?

SHEILA: Don't you click your fingers at me! We're losing. I can tell that much.

HARRY: Very helpful.

SHEILA: Well, for heaven's sake, you're supposed to be keeping it!

HARRY: Let's see ... it's your serve ...

SHEILA: I know we've won two games ...

HARRY: And I started serving this set ...

SHEILA: I *think* it's two – five. *(She indicates her side and opponents' side of net.)*

HARRY: Hell, really? *(Turns front.)* Know the score, Jim? ... Two – *four*!

1	**score** [skɔ:]	number of points made in a game
6	floats [fləʊts]	footlights; the lights at the front of the stage
7	**a racket** ['rækɪt]	the instrument used for hitting a tennis ball
	to mime s.th.	to simulate s.th. through gestures
8	a game [geɪm]	a single part of a set *(Satz)* in tennis
10	to lull s.o. [lʌl]	to cause s.o. to become sleepy or less attentive
12	upstage	at the back of the stage *(Bühne)*
13	a query ['kwɪərɪ]	a question
19	a serve	the act of serving the ball, i.e. putting it into play

... No, no. *(Pleased)* If you say so – we've – er – we've lost count! *(Traps ball from* JIM.*)* Thanks! *(Traps ball from* JANE *right.)* Grazie *(pronounced Grahtsy-eh)* Jane! Sheila's serve! *(Throws ball back in general direction of* SHEILA.*)* Put it on his backhand. *(Settles and smiles at* JANE.*)*

(Slight pause. SHEILA *is getting her hair in place, then collects two balls and comes to baseline to serve.)*

(To JANE*)* Sorry, was I staring? ... Oh! Your hair! I thought you said my ... I think it looks wonderful ... I wish you'd tell Sheila where you go: she has such a terrible time keeping it even presentable! ... Oh yes, the hair's all right – it's what she does with it, poor darling.

*(*SHEILA *serves.* HARRY *misses* JIM'S *return.)*

Damn! Good shot, Jim! *(To* JANE*)* Better keep my eye on the *ball*! *(To* SHEILA*)* I said his *back*hand!

SHEILA *(calm)*: It was the wind.

HARRY: Oh. *(Then, realising)* There's not a *breath* of wind!

(He has crossed down right. SHEILA *collects balls on way up left.)*

SHEILA: Love – fifteen.

*(*SHEILA *serves. Into the net.* HARRY *picks it up quickly. On* SHEILA'S *second serve* HARRY *misses* JANE'S *sideline return.)*

(Sweetly) Wouldn't you be more use back here, darling?

HARRY: Server's partner always stands at the net.

SHEILA: Only when he can make contact with the occasional ball, surely.

*(*SHEILA *goes right to pick up ball.* HARRY *crosses down left and talks across right to* JANE.*)*

HARRY: Afraid we're not giving you much of a match, Jane ... Oh, well, if you play every week! ... No, Sheila always seems to have so much to do – in the house ... Oh yes, au-pairs – they never stay, though.

SHEILA: Love – thirty.

HARRY: We've a Belgian girl at the moment ...

SHEILA: You'll get hurt, Harry, if you stand so far over as that!

HARRY *(moving left but continuing talking to* JANE*)*: But I caught *her*

1	to trap s.th.	*here:* to catch s.th.
6	baseline ['beɪslaɪn]	line marking the limit of play at each end of a tennis court
16	down right	to the right of the stage (from the actor's point of view)
17	love	zero (in tennis)
19	sideline ['saɪdlaɪn]	line marking the limit of play at the side of a tennis court
24	au pair [ˌəʊ'peə]	

looking up the cross-Channel ferries yesterday.
*(*SHEILA *serves. Into the net.* HARRY *picks up the ball.)*
Sheila just can't get on with them.
*(*SHEILA *serves again. Into net.* HARRY *picks it up.)*
Double.

SHEILA *(cutting but smiling)*: Yes, I saw.

HARRY *(to* JANE*)*: *I* find them – stimulating. They keep you young!

SHEILA: Balls; please. *(She is up left.)*
(HARRY *bounces the two balls he has in his hand back to her.)*
Love – forty.
*(*SHEILA *serves.* HARRY *takes vicious swipe at the return and wins the point.)*

HARRY: Grazie, Jim, it wasn't too bad, was it!

SHEILA: Fifteen – forty.
*(*HARRY *hasn't moved.)*
(Repeats) Fifteen – forty. *(Pause.)* Other side, Harry.

HARRY: Oh. *(Moves left, speaks right to* JANE.*)* That's my best shot – I've been trying to get it back all day!
*(*SHEILA *serves. It hits* HARRY *on the neck.)*
Ow!

SHEILA: I warned you – you were practically on the centre line!

HARRY *(to* JANE*)*: I suppose that's what they call a lethal serve.
*(*HARRY *moves further left.* SHEILA *serves. The return goes to her and she drives to* JANE. HARRY *repeats his swipe and wins the point.)*
That's better! *(Crossing right.) Thirty* – forty! Now, we need a couple more like that ...

SHEILA: *I* need something to serve with.

HARRY: Eh? Oh ... *(Starts looking for balls.)*

SHEILA *(trapping one and then another from* JIM*)*: Thank you, Jim. *(Low)* Glad someone has some manners.

HARRY: Oh, stop nagging.

5	double (fault)	two serving faults one after the other (giving a point to the opponents)
6	cutting	*here:* sarcastic
8	balls	*here possibly slang for:* rubbish
9	to bounce a ball [baʊns]	to make a ball spring up by hitting it against the ground
11	**vicious** ['vɪʃəs]	violent, dangerous
	swipe [swaɪp]	a forceful sweeping blow
19	Ow! [aʊ]	exclamation of pain
21	lethal ['li:θəl]	causing death, deadly; *here:* very dangerous
30	to nag	to find fault or complain continuously

SHEILA: Thirty – forty, then.

(She serves from up left. HARRY *takes third swipe, grins delightedly at the result and starts to turn upstage.)*

HARRY: Deuce! *(Stops centre and turns to* JIM.*) Out?! (Looks at* SHEILA.*)* Out?! *(Then back at* JIM.*)* Are you sure, Jim? ... No, no, I just thought ... Oh, thanks, Jane, no, there's no need to play it again – if *you* say ... *(Slight pause.)* I must admit I thought ...

SHEILA: Don't argue, Harry.

(HARRY *moves back towards* SHEILA.)

SHEILA: Your game, then ... *(She hits ball across to* JANE. *Turns to* HARRY.*)* Five – two.

HARRY: Did it look out to you?

SHEILA: Couldn't possibly tell from back here. I take Jim's word.

HARRY: You would. *(Throws a couple of balls over net from baseline.)* Your serve, Jane.

SHEILA: Don't know what's worrying you. Thought you wanted them to win.

HARRY: What on earth are you talking about?

SHEILA: You said it might make things easier at the office ...

HARRY: If we didn't beat them by too wide a margin, you idiot! I never said ...

SHEILA: Well, that's not very likely, is it, the way you're playing!

HARRY: And you're Virginia Wade, I suppose! If you're so ...

SHEILA: What were you nattering to Jane about?

HARRY: Oh, this and that ... What Jim? Oh yes, we're ready.

SHEILA: You'd do better to concentrate on the game. Tennis.

HARRY *(to* JIM*)*: Just a little conference on tactics. *(Moves to net left.)* Yes, Jane: five – two ... Cinque – due *(Cheenkweh – Dooeh.)*

SHEILA *(mutters)*: Eight days in San Remo ...

(SHEILA *receives serve. Her return is smashed by* JIM.*)*

4	deuce [dju:s]	(in tennis) 40–40
	Stops centre.	He stops at the centre.
14	You would.	That's typical of you; that's what I expected you to do.
20	a wide margin ['mɑ:dʒɪn]	*here:* a big difference (in score)
23	Virginia Wade	one of the best-known British women tennis players (some years ago)
24	to natter *(coll.)*	to talk continuously about unimportant things; to chatter
29	**to mutter**	to speak in a low voice, not easily heard, under one's breath

HARRY: Shot, Jim! *(To* SHEILA*)* You gave it to him on a plate!

SHEILA: Couldn't help it – my racket slipped.

HARRY: That's just your trouble – you don't use the right grip. Your racket can't slip if you hold it properly: like this. *(He demonstrates.)* Look – *you* hold it like *this*!

SHEILA: Who's nagging now? ... Here you are, Jane! *(Throws ball across and moves down right to net position and talks across to* JIM *left.)* What, Jim? ... Oh, do you think so? *(Looks down at, smoothes her dress.)* How nice of you to say ... Heavens no, I made it myself, from a pattern ... I'm lucky to be able to buy darning wool on the dress allowance Harry gives me ... I'm always green with envy at Jane's clothes.

*(*HARRY *receives* JANE'S *serve. His return is smashed by* JIM.*)*

SHEILA: What was that about handing it on a plate?

HARRY: It was Jane's serve. It was a brute! ... Lovely serve, Janey!

SHEILA: Janey? Since when Janey?

HARRY: Everyone calls her that.

SHEILA: I don't.

HARRY: Come on ... it's thirty – love.

(SHEILA, *up right, returns* JANE'S *serve.*)

Well done.

*(*HARRY, *at net left, returns next shot,* SHEILA *the next, but when ball comes back fourth time,* HARRY *makes attempt to stretch across right.)*

All right, mine! *(Misses it.)* No – yours!

(But SHEILA *has changed courts by now and can't retrieve* HARRY'S *miss.)*

SHEILA: Oh charming! I could have got it perfectly well if you ...

HARRY *(becoming more and more tense)*: Then why didn't you!

(He picks up two balls at baseline and smashes them across net. SHEILA *walks to position at net right.)*

1	to give s.o. s.th. on a plate	to allow s.o. to get s.th. without effort
2	**to slip**	to slide out of position
8	**to smooth s.th.** [smu:ð]	to make s.th. smooth; to make the surface of s.th. flat and even
9	**a pattern** ['pætən]	*Muster*
10	darning wool ['dɑ:nɪŋ ˌwu:l]	wool used for repairing holes in stockings or socks
	an allowance [ə'laʊəns]	an amount of money given regularly for a special purpose
12	to smash the ball	to hit the ball powerfully
14	Sheila has changed courts. [kɔ:ts]	Sheila has run to another part of the tennis court.
	to retrieve a miss [rɪ'tri:v]	to return a ball that has been missed
26	tense [tens]	nervous

SHEILA: Calm down, darling, it's only a game. *(To* JIM*)* Honestly, I don't know what's the matter with Harry today – he's right off ... Yes, he should, you're right ... It's all I can do to get him out to post a letter sometimes ... He comes back from the office and just slumps in a chair watching television ... *(Laughs.)* Oh yes, he always watches Wimbledon ... you'd never have guessed it, would you!

HARRY: Sheila! It's forty – love! Match point!

SHEILA: Well, try not to send this one straight to Jimmy ... *(Smiles at* JIM.*)* He's got a terrific smash.

HARRY: Got a terrific what?

SHEILA *(dry and clipped)*: Smash.

*(*HARRY *returns* JANE'S *serve* to JANE. *Ball comes back to* SHEILA *who plays it to* JIM. JIM *smashes to* HARRY *who, wide left, gets it back to* JANE. JANE'S *shot comes back very high and* SHEILA *starts to run backwards.)*

All right!

HARRY: *I* can!

(He hopping sideways from left, she hopping backwards from right, eyes on the high ball, bump and land on their knees. Then the ball lands on HARRY'S *head.)*

Typical! Is there nothing you can do right?!

SHEILA: Oh, Harry – for God's sake ...

HARRY: I had a chance at a beautiful shot, so of course I get knocked out of the way. Hell, Sheila, it's not as if you were good at anything else – it's the same casual, half-hearted, sloppy approach to everything that makes you such a mess as a person!

SHEILA: My approach ...

HARRY: It's only a game! Isn't that what you said? Only a game! So that means you don't have to put anything into it – just slop along and titter when you make a complete fool of yourself – and me – *(Turning still full of anger.)* Yes Jim, what is it?!

2	right off	not as good as usual at all
4	to slump [slʌmp]	to fall down heavily
7	match point	final point needed to win a tennis match
11	clipped [klɪpt]	short-spoken, abrupt
18	to bump	to collide, to crash together
24	**casual** ['kæʒʊəl]	careless, indifferent
	sloppy ['slɒpɪ]	very careless
25	a mess [mes]	*here:* someone untidy and disorderly
28	to slop along	to move about in a lazy, purposeless way
	to titter ['tɪtə]	to laugh in a silly or nervous way

SHEILA: He said it's only a game.

(Pause while HARRY *looks at each of them, calms himself, and musters a smile.)*

HARRY: Well, I suppose we should be thankful there are no bones broken! Well! Game, set and match! *(Approaches net.)* Well played you two!

SHEILA: Beaten fair and square.

HARRY *(to* JANE*)*: Mmm .. No, no – please go on, Jane – I'm always glad to learn from an expert ... How do you mean, my grip? ... Oh yes? ... Well ... I must try to remember that *(Trying it.)* Yes ... see that, darling?

SHEILA *(mild)*: Yes.

HARRY: Thank you, Jane ...

SHEILA *(to* JIM*)*: No, we're in no hurry, are we, Harry.

HARRY: No ... Lovely! But I insist on buying them ... No, Jim, I insist! ... No. I'm not going to have you buying ...

SHEILA *(interrupts)*: Well, the *second* round, then. Come on, Harry, help me collect the balls.

HARRY *(to* JIM *and* JANE*)*: No, you go ahead – we'll be right with you.

*(*HARRY *moves to help* SHEILA*. They both stop and look after their departing opponents.)*

(Sighing): I suppose we need more practice.

SHEILA: Intensive training, if you're hoping tennis will help your career.

HARRY: Sorry, darling.

SHEILA: It's all right. There are some behind you. *(He leaves her.)* If only you didn't get so het up!

HARRY: Maybe I should take up bridge – not half as exhausting.

SHEILA: You'd be that much closer to Janey at the card table.

HARRY: You *jealous?*

SHEILA: Oh, now, Harry, darling, please. Even you can't seriously think you'd get anywhere with *that* one. How could I possibly be jealous?

HARRY: Oh.

SHEILA: Besides, you can tell they're both mad about each other.

HARRY: Yes ... I must admit, I see Jim's point! She's quite a girl.

2	to muster a smile ['mʌstə]	to manage to smile
5	game, set and match	said when the final point in the whole game is won
6	fair and square [skweə]	without any doubt; completely
24	het up *(coll.)*	angry, excited
25	bridge	a card game for four players
	exhausting [ɪg'zɔ:stɪŋ]	tiring
27	**jealous** ['dʒeləs]	angry or afraid that someone who should love you loves s.o. else better *(eifersüchtig)*

SHEILA: Oh, I never denied that – they're a very handsome couple.

HARRY *(thinking of* JANE*)*: Beautiful.

SHEILA: The trouble is, they *know* it. *(Points.)* There's one over there. And all the time she must spend – to say nothing of money – keeping up that glossy look ... lovely, I know – but is it *worth* it!

HARRY: I imagine Jim thinks so. Of course, he's the brainy one of the two – brilliant at the office, you know. I really wasn't jealous when he was promoted – he deserved it.

SHEILA: He always gives me the feeling of pressure ... that his brain's ticking away ...

HARRY: Yes ... Well, let's face it, you can be too clever, can't you. I mean ... it's brought him a good job and wonderful prospects – but the strain of always keeping one jump ahead – trying to outguess everyone else – I don't think I could live like that.

SHEILA: No ...

HARRY: That the lot?

SHEILA *(She glances into the box he holds.)*: Six. Yes.

HARRY: Come along then, Miss Wade ...

SHEILA: Yes, Mr Laver – or may I call you 'Rod'?

(They move downstage to follow JIM *and* JANE.*)*

HARRY *(Stops.)*: Yes ... they may be attractive, and clever, successful, well-adjusted ... and happy ... but don't let's fool ourselves, there's more to life than that, isn't there.

*(*SHEILA *turns to look at him as* BLACKOUT.*)*

5	glossy ['glɒsi]	shiny and smooth; attractive and stylish
6	brainy *(coll.)*	intelligent; having brains
10	to tick away	to make a sound like a clock
12	prospects ['prɒspekts]	chances of success (in one's career)
	strain [streɪn]	pressure, stress, tension
13	to outguess s.o.	to be better at guessing than s.o.
16	That the lot?	Is that all?
19	Rod Laver	a well-known Australian tennis champion (some years ago)
22	well-adjusted	well-balanced emotionally

By courtesy of Lyndon Brook

Biographical Notes

Lyndon Brook was born in America in 1926. He has lived in Britain since 1942. He is not only a playwright but also an actor. His plays comprise historical dramas (*Fool's Mate,* 1953 and *Rogue Prince,* 1958) as well as thrillers (*Love Her to Death!*, 1955 and *The Uninvited Host,* 1964).

Score was published in a collection of short plays ('Mixed Doubles') in 1970. In this play a married couple tries very hard to be equal to or better than their successful and attractive opponents – not only in tennis but also in life.

Unterrichtsvorschläge

Vorbemerkungen

1. Inhalt

Harry und Sheila spielen gerade mit Jim und Jane eine gemischtes Doppel. Sie befinden sich im letzten Satz ihres Tennisspiels und sind eindeutig auf der Verliererstraße. Der Grund liegt auf der Hand: Harry und Sheila sind einfach zu schlechte Tennisspieler, als daß sie Jim und Jane überhaupt gefährden könnten. Ihre Aufschläge und Returns sind miserabel, sie verfehlen Bälle, sie sind vielfach ungünstig postiert oder spielen ihren Gegnern die Bälle so zu, daß diese ihre Punkte leicht mit Schmetterbällen holen können. Der ihre Niederlage besiegelnde Matchball erreicht beide schließlich in einer symbolisch-lächerlichen Situation: Harry und Sheila landen auf den Knien, der Ball selbst auf Harrys Kopf.

Eigentlich war es Harrys Absicht gewesen, Jim, seinen äußerst erfolgreichen Kollegen, und dessen Partnerin Jane wenigstens einmal auf sportlichem Feld zu schlagen, und zwar „großzügigerweise" mit nicht zu deutlichem Abstand (**39** 20). Aber die Realität hat diese Wunschvorstellung längst ein- bzw. überholt. Harry befindet sich plötzlich unter dem fatalen Zwang, angesichts des sportlichen Fiaskos wenigstens sein Gesicht nicht zu verlieren. Er fängt nicht nur an, schrecklich anzugeben und das „miserable" Spiel seiner Partnerin zu kritisieren, er wird ihr gegenüber auch zunehmend unhöflicher, unfreundlicher und besonders in den Situationen verletzend, in denen er Janes Vorzüge vergleichend herausstellt. Schließlich steht er dermaßen unter Wettbewerbsdruck, daß er völlig außer Fassung gerät, offen aggressiv wird und das Tennisspiel als völligen Ernst auffaßt. Seine Partnerin Sheila kann seinem Druck nur dadurch standhalten, daß für sie das Spiel aufgrund ihres Realitätssinns immer noch ein Spiel bleibt.

Nachdem die imaginären Gegner das Spielfeld verlassen haben, sammeln Harry und Sheila die Bälle auf. Es kommt zu einer Art „Bestandsaufnahme": Beide merken, wie leicht man sich in einer Konkurrenzsituation zum Narren machen kann. Sie erkennen, daß Jim und Jane als erfolgreiches, schönes, bewundertes Paar (**43** 21) ständig am „Ball" bleiben und ihre ganze Energie darauf verwenden müssen, im Konkurrenzkampf des Lebens zu bestehen. Harry und Sheila bescheiden sich. Aus ihrer Niederlage ziehen sie schließlich den Erkenntnisgewinn, daß Erfolg sehr relativ sein kann und daß es mehr und anderes im Leben gibt, als irgendwelchen Erfolgserlebnissen nachzujagen ('Don't let's fool ourselves, there's more to life than that' **43** 22–23).

Bemerkenswert ist die besondere Struktur des Dramas. Lediglich Harry und Sheila werden auf der Bühne dargestellt. Sie wenden sich in ihren

Kommentaren, Fragen und Antworten agierend und reagierend an Jim und Jane, die jenseits des quer über die Vorderbühne gespannten Tennisnetzes – auf der Seite der Zuschauer – spielen. Das bedeutet, daß die auf der Seite der Gewinner sitzenden Zuschauer ständig in das Spiel hineingezogen werden. Sie sind gehalten, gewissermaßen mitzuspielen, indem sie den gesamten dramatischen Ablauf (Dialoge, Aktionen) durch eigene Phantasie und Vorstellung fortlaufend ergänzen müssen.

2. Thematische Aspekte

Die in *Score* aufgeworfene Problematik ermöglicht die Zuordnung des Werks zu Unterrichtsreihen über *sports,* bzw. zu solchen, in denen Begriffe wie *success, competition (in society), appearance and reality, winning and losing, loss of identity,* und *the meaning of life* angesprochen werden. Darüberhinaus ist das Werk durch seine Struktur von besonderem gattungsspezifischem Reiz.

3. Methodische Hinweise

Das Drama ist in zwei Teile gegliedert: Der erste Teil (**36** 1–**42** 6) schildert den Weg Harrys und Sheilas bis zu ihrer Niederlage, der zweite Teil (**42** 20–**43** 24) stellt – nach einem kurzen Zwischenteil (**42** 7–**42** 19) – ihre Reflexion über das gegnerische Paar dar. Die folgenden Unterrichtsvorschläge beziehen sich auf diesen Aufbau und sind als „Angebot" zu verstehen. Sie bieten Hilfen für vorbereitende Informationen, für lektürebegleitende Aufgaben, für Fragestellungen zur Analyse und für Aspekte der Evaluation. Sie sollen durch Übersichten, Tafelskizzen und schüleraktivierende Aufgaben ein methodisch variantenreiches (intensives und extensives) Vorgehen ermöglichen.

Ein wichtiger Hinweis zum Einsatz der Cassette: Obwohl die Spieldauer der Cassette nur ca. 11 Minuten beträgt, ist ein **auditiver Einstieg** (Hörverständnis) in die Lektüre des Dramas **nicht ratsam.** Erfahrungsgemäß sind die Schüler überfordert, wenn sie die Rollen von Harry und Sheila hören und verstehen, sich darüberhinaus die imaginären Aussagen von Jim und Jane vorstellen und dann auch noch den Ablauf des Tennisspiels erfassen sollen. Hier bedarf es eines behutsamen Heranführens zum Text durch vorbereitende Informationen und eine schrittweise Lektüre, in deren Rahmen dann die Tonaufnahme sinnvoll ergänzend eingesetzt werden kann.

Unit 1: Suggested Pre-reading Activities

Die Lektüre des Dramas sollte durch eine Reihe von vorentlastenden Hinweisen und Tafeldiagrammen vorbereitet werden.

1. A tennis court

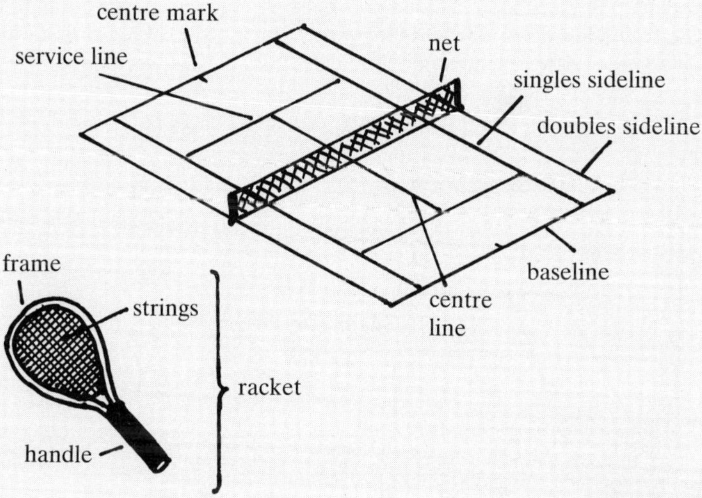

2. The most important tennis rules

Scoring:
A tennis **match** is divided into **sets,** and a set is divided into **games.**
The points in a game are scored as follows:
1st point: 15
2nd point: 30
3rd point: 40
4th point: game
The side that first wins the 4th point wins the **game,** unless the score is 40:40 (deuce). (In this case, the first side to be two points ahead of the opponent wins the game.) The first side to win six games wins the **set,** unless the score is 5:5. (In this case, again, the first side to be two points ahead wins the set.)

The side that wins two out of three sets wins the **match.**

Serving and returning:
A game is started by a player standing on the right-hand side behind the baseline, who **serves** the ball over the net into the diagonally opposite service court (the rectangle next to the net). The ball has then to be **returned** by the opponent, and has to be returned again by the serving side, etc.

If the server makes two serving mistakes one after the other (a double fault), the other side wins a point.

A point is given to the other side if a player fails to return the ball correctly or sends it outside the opponent's court (if the ball is 'out').

After each point has been decided on, the server changes from the right-hand side to the left-hand side and vice versa. One player serves during the whole of a game. After each game the players take turns at serving.

3. Introduction of the main characters

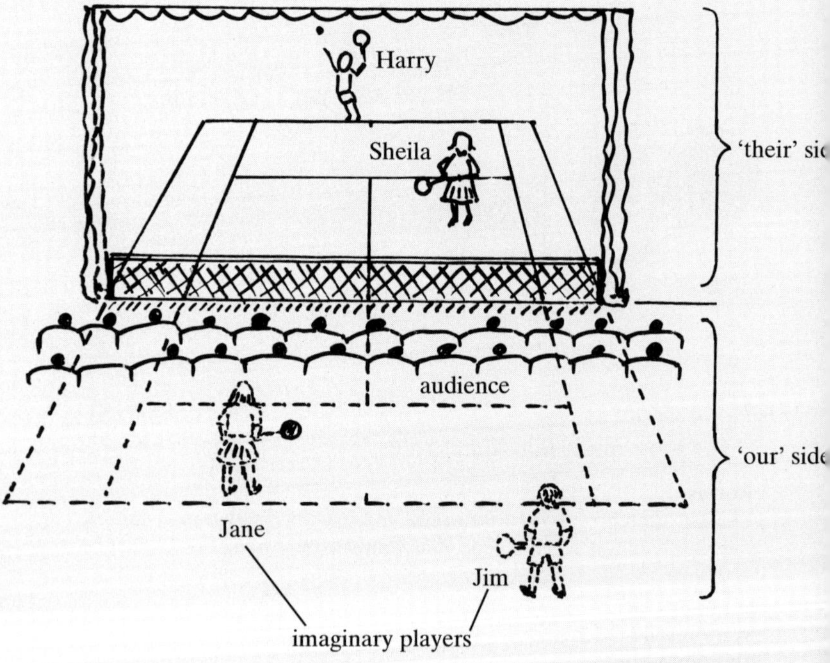

The audience is supposed to take an active part in the game, since the words and actions of Jim and Jane must be constantly inferred from Harry's and Sheila's **re**actions to what their opponents apparently do and say. (It can be compared to a telephone call on the stage).

4. Acting areas on the stage

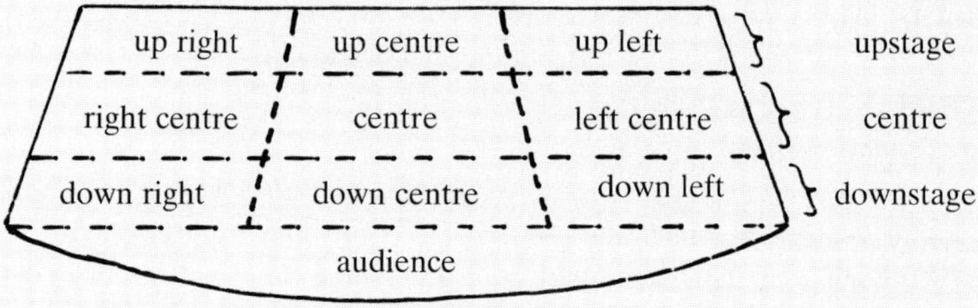

Unit 2: Reading the Text

Es empfiehlt sich eine schrittweise Lektüre des Texts unter Einbeziehung der Cassette, wobei das Anhören der Aufnahme immer dann unterbrochen werden sollte, wenn längere Regieanweisungen gelesen werden müssen. Die Aufnahme berücksichtigt nur die Dialogteile und einige wenige akustische Signale, die den Ablauf des Tennisspiels verdeutlichen.

Darüberhinaus sollte man unbedingt an den Stellen innehalten, an denen die Dialogteile mit dem imaginären Gegner angedeutet werden. Es wäre günstig, wenn einige dieser Abschnitte exemplarisch ergänzt werden könnten (u. U. mit einem Arbeitsauftrag).

Classroom assignment

1. *Write down what Jim might be saying to Harry in the pauses.*

*a) p.***36** *1.24 – p.***37** *1.2.*

HARRY: Hell, really?
Know the score, Jim?

← **JIM:** Oh yes; it's four – two to us, and Sheila's serve, so 2–4 to you.

Two – *four?*

← **JIM:** Yes, that's right. You and Sheila have won two games and we've won 4. Did Sheila think ...?

No, no. If you say so ...

*b) p.**37** l.7–10.*

← **JANE:** *(sotto voce):* Poor girl – always having trouble with her hair.

HARRY: Sorry, was I staring? *(He misunderstands.)*

← **JANE:** No, no, I was talking about my hair. *(She covers up.)*

HARRY: Oh, your hair. I thought you said my ...

← **JANE:** Do you like the way I've had it cut?

HARRY: I think it looks wonderful ...

← **JANE:** Thank you. Glad you like it.

HARRY: I wish you'd tell Sheila where you go: she has such a terrible time keeping it even presentable!

← **JANE:** But she's got lovely hair ...

HARRY: Oh yes, the hair's all right – it's what she does with it, poor darling.

c) Suggestions for further passages to be completed: **37** 25–27; **40** 7–11; **41** 1–6; **42** 7–9; **42** 11–17

2. *Imagine you are the producer of the play: if your audience are not likely to know who Virginia Wade (**39** 23) and Rod Laver (**43** 19) are – or rather were –, which tennis champions would you put in their place?*

Classroom assignment or homework:

3. *How do Harry and Sheila lose the match? Describe the course of the play by making a diagram.*

Suggested diagram:

The beginning of the drama

FINAL SET

GAMES: 2–4

Sheila serves. Jim returns the ball. Harry misses it.	0:15	Jane and Jim (Harry and Sheila's imaginary opponents)
Sheila serves it into the net. Sheila's second service is returned by Jane. Harry misses Jane's sideline return.	0:30	
Sheila serves into the net twice (double fault).	0:40	
Sheila serves. Harry takes vicious swipe at the return and wins the point.	15:40	
Sheila serves. Ball hits Harry on the neck. Sheila serves again. Return goes to her. She drives ball to Jane. Harry repeats his swipe and wins the point.	30:40	
Sheila serves. Harry takes third swipe – thinks he's won the point (Deuce?). But in fact it is out.	game	

GAMES: 2–5

Sheila receives serve. Her return is smashed by Jim.	0:15	Jane and Jim (Harry and Sheila's imaginary opponents)
Harry receives Jane's serve. His return is smashed by Jim.	0:30	
Sheila returns Jane's serve. Harry returns next shot, Sheila the next. Misunderstanding: Harry tries to get it, misses it and tells Sheila to get it. Sheila can't retrieve his miss.	0:40	
Harry returns Jane's serve to Jane, Jane – Sheila – Jim smashes it to Harry – Jane (very high shot), Harry and Sheila bump and land on knees. Ball lands on Harry's head.	game	

GAME – SET – MATCH

4. *Describe Harry and Sheila's tennis skills.*
Sheila and Harry are not good at tennis. Harry keeps missing the ball and Sheila serves badly. One of Sheila's serves even hits Harry on the neck. Their returns are poor: they are either 'out' or Harry and Sheila hand them to their opponents 'on a plate'. They play 10 points during the play, but win only two of them (only two of Harry's 'swipes' (= volleys) are successful). They also lose points because of misunderstandings about who is going to take the ball.
Their defeat is utter mockery: they finally land on their knees with the ball bouncing on Harry's head.

Unit 3: Analysis of the Play

Das Gespräch über die psychologische Situation der beiden Spieler auf der Bühne kann durch folgende Fragen angeregt werden, wobei die Möglichkeit besteht, die Fragen auch durch ein Studium der jeweils angegebenen Textstellen selbständig beantworten zu lassen (Arbeitsaufträge).

1. *What does Harry hope he will achieve by playing tennis with Jim? (Refer to **39** 16–21; **42** 21; **43** 6–8.)*
Harry plays tennis with Jim in order to make Jim put in a good word for him at the office. Harry knows that Jim is brilliant at the office and that he got promotion much sooner than he did himself (**43** 6–8). Harry must admit that Jim deserved it and he even emphasizes that he 'really wasn't jealous'. Now he is 'forced' to praise Jim's skill at tennis. His intention was to beat Jim, but not 'by not too wide a margin' (**39** 20).

He hoped that things would be made easier at the office then. But now his plans fail and his hopes are disappointed. He misses his chance of being accepted as an equal (or even better) opponent, which is very difficult to bear.

2. *Harry and Sheila not only have difficulty in accepting their defeat, but also find each other's tennis irritating. Give examples. (Refer to the text from **36** 14 to **41** 20.)*
At the beginning Harry and Sheila are busy coping with their lack of skill and their incompetence. First they lose count. They obviously find it difficult to keep the score, which probably would not happen to players who are about to win (**36** 14/24; **37** 1). Later on Harry doubts whether his ball is 'out' and cannot really get over the fact that this **is** the case ... according to Jim (**39** 4–7/12). Sheila on the other hand blames her bad performance on the wind (but funnily enough, there is no wind; **37** 14–15) and on her racket, which 'slipped' (**40** 2). Apparently she expects everybody – and especially Harry – to find no fault in her own play. In addition to this, throughout the

play Harry and Sheila keep telling each other how to play: how to hold the racket (**40** 3–5), how to place the ball and who to play it to (**37** 4/13;**41** 8), and where to stand (**37** 20/30). They also blame each other unfairly and criticize each other's performance (**37** 22; **38** 20; **39** 22–23; **40** 13/25–26; **41** 20–23). Each of them wants to appear to be better than the other and to have a superior knowledge of the game and its tactics. At the same time each shows intense irritation at the other's style of play.

Suggestions for the blackboard:

Harry	Sheila
have difficulty in accepting their defeat	
● loses count (**36** 14/24; **37** 1)	● loses count (**36** 22)
● doubts whether ball is 'out' (**39** 5–7/12)	● tries to blame bad performance on – the wind (**37** 14) – her racket (it 'slipped') (**40** 2)
find each other's tennis irritating	
● they tell each other what to do	
– 'Put it on his backhand.' (**37** 4/13) – 'Server's partner always stands at the net.' (**37** 21) – demonstrates how to hold a racket (**40** 3–5)	– 'Wouldn't you be more use back here, darling?' (**37** 20) – 'You'll get hurt, Harry, if you stand as far over as that!' (**37** 30)
● they blame and criticize each other	
– 'And you're Virginia Wade, I suppose!' (**39** 23) – 'You gave it to him on a plate!' (**40** 1)	– 'I warned you – you were practically on the centre line!' (**38** 20) – '... the way you're playing!' (**39** 22) – 'I could have got it perfectly well if you ...' (**40** 25)

3. *Describe the psychological relationship between Harry and Sheila during the match. Is it only each other's tennis that Harry and Sheila find irritating?*
There is mounting tension between Harry and Sheila, obviously caused by the fact that their nerves are strained. They exert all their energies on not losing face because they both know they are going to lose the game. Harry

can only rid himself of his tension by being rude, unfair and unfriendly. In fact, he behaves very badly indeed. He insults Sheila, who finally becomes the object of his uncontrolled anger. He is furious with her and tells her that she is 'such a mess as a person' (**41** 25) and that she always makes a complete fool of herself (**41** 29). For Harry the game of tennis is no longer just a game. He loses control and attacks Sheila viciously.

Sheila on the other hand gets rid of her tension in a more or less subtle way. She **re**acts rather than acts, by commenting on Harry's use of Italian (she mutters only; **39** 28–29). Her tone of voice is varied and often disguises her feelings: She speaks sweetly (**37** 20), in a cutting way although still smiling (**38** 6), in a dry and clipped way (**41** 11) and in a mild way (**42** 10). Somehow she tries to keep her composure yet sometimes cannot help reacting with outright aggression, especially when Harry treats her like someone he can click his fingers at (**36** 15). When Harry attacks her sharply, she realizes that Harry is making a fool of himself. She therefore tries to calm him by saying that it is only a game (**41** 1).

Suggestions for the blackboard:

Harry		Sheila
• *is impolite:* clicks his fingers at Sheila (**36** 13)	T	• *reacts aggressively:* 'Don't you click your fingers at me!' (**36** 15)
• *is sarcastic:* 'Very helpful.' (**36** 17)	E N	• *artificial friendliness:* '*(Sweetly)* Wouldn't you be more use back here, darling?' (**37** 20)
	→ S ←	'*(Cutting but smiling):* Yes, I saw.' (**38** 6)
• *is quick to point out her shortcomings:* 'Double.' (**38** 5)	I	
• *insults Sheila:* 'Oh, stop nagging.' (**38** 30) '... you idiot!' (**39** 20)	O	• *cuts Harry short:* 'Balls' (= nonsense) (**38** 8)
	N	• *comments on his Italian:* 'Eight days in San Remo ...' (**39** 29)
⬇		⬇
• **is full of anger**		• **shows mild reaction**
You are 'such a mess as a person!' (**41** 25) 'you make a complete fool of yourself' (**41** 29) ⟩	⇦	'Calm down, darling, it's only a game!' (**41** 1)
For Harry it's no longer a game. (He is making a complete fool of himself.)		For Sheila it still is only a game.

4. *Describe the relationship between Harry and Jane.*
Harry is just losing the game of tennis, which he regards as a stain on his reputation. Therefore he feels the urge to show himself in a favourable light in order not to lose face. He tries to make himself popular with Jane and to improve his image. He shows off by trying to impress Jane with his skill and intelligence. Ironically enough, his skill is limited to two successful smashes and his intelligence seems to be embarrassingly reduced to a few bits of Italian *(grazie, cinque, due;* **38** 12; **39** 28). He is also willing to 'yield' to Jane's authority: not only does he admire her play ('It was a brute! ... Lovely serve'; **40** 14), but also accepts her decision that the ball was out (**39** 6) and her instructions on how to hold the racket (**42** 7–9). He is grateful for her advice, which reveals – psychologically speaking – a kind of submissiveness. In addition, Harry is unfair and insincere in that he flatters Jane at Sheila's expense. Apparently he wants to gain advantage from making comparisons. He admires Jane's hair and criticizes Sheila's (**37** 7–10), he apologizes for their bad performance – blaming it on Sheila (**37** 25–27). He also curries favour by calling Jane 'Janey' (**40** 14) and flings an indirect, nasty insult at Sheila by telling Jane that he finds au-pair girls 'stimulating' (**38** 7).

Harry's showing off, his feigned submissiveness as well as his attempt at gaining advantage from comparisons and at showing a certain kind of 'machismo' can be regarded as the consequences of the competitive situation. He allows himself to exhibit this strange behaviour because he doesn't want to admit to being the loser.

5. *How does Sheila react?*
Sheila's reaction to Harry's 'billing and cooing' is comparatively mild. Due to her sense of reality she knows that even Harry himself would never seriously think he is a match for Jane. She sticks to the facts: she and Harry are just losing the game. Therefore she only asks Harry to concentrate on the game (**39** 26) and occasionally cuts him short ('Balls'; **38** 8), dismissing his conversation with Jane as nonsense. Only when Harry calls Jane 'Janey' does she begin to get angry and a little jealous.

The serve that hits Harry on the neck (**38** 18) can be considered as a symbolical incident: he pushes himself to the forefront even on the tennis court – and is hit by Sheila (which he ironically describes as 'a lethal serve'; **38** 21), who wants to get him back under control.

Answers to question 5 and 6 can be summed up on the board as follows (see overleaf):

Harry (⟶ Jane)

- *shows off:*
  says 'Grazie' (**37** 2), 'Cinque – due' (**39** 28)
  shows pride: 'That's my best shot' (**38** 16)
- *admires Jane's tennis playing:*
  'It was a brute! ... Lovely serve' (**40** 14)
- *accepts ...*
  ... Jane's decision: ball 'out' (**39** 6)
  ... being instructed (how to hold the racket) (**42** 7–9)

} Harry tries to improve his image

- *tries to flatter Jane at Sheila's expense:*
  - admires Jane's hair (**37** 8–10) (Sheila 'has such a terrible time keeping it even presentable!')
  - apologizes for bad performance (blames it on Sheila) (**37** 25–27)
- *tells Jane that au-pairs are stimulating and that they keep him young* (**38** 7)
- *calls Jane 'Janey'* (**40** 14)

Sheila's reaction

- *blames Harry:*
  'You'd do better to concentrate on the game. Tennis.' (**39** 26)
- *cuts Harry short*
  - 'Balls' (**38** 8)
  - 'What were you nattering to Jane about?' (**39** 24)
- *gets angry/a little jealous*
  'Since when Janey?' (**40** 15)

6. *What do Sheila's 'dialogues' with Jim reveal about herself and Harry? (**40** 7–11 and **41** 1–6)*

In contrast to Jane, Sheila must make her dresses herself, from patterns (**40** 9), and although her home-made dress is admired by Jim, she envies Jane her stylish appearance. At least that's what she tells Jim ('I'm always green with envy at Jane's clothes'; **40** 11). Later on the audience (the reader) will find out that she thinks that Jane's appearance is of debatable value, since she must spend a lot of time (let alone money) to keep up 'that glossy look' (**43** 4–5). In addition, Harry is criticized indirectly and compared with Jim: Jim is a player with 'a terrific smash' (**41** 9), whose word can be believed ('I take Jim's word'; **39**, 13) and who has good manners (**38** 29). Harry on the other hand is shown as a terrible miser (cf the insufficient 'dress allowance' he gives her; **40** 10) and as someone who is lazy and does nothing but watch TV (ironically, he always watches Wimbledon; **41** 5).

7. *Do Harry and Sheila admit their defeat?*

To a certain extent Harry and Sheila are good losers in that they admit their defeat. Harry's words 'Well! Game, set and match! Well played you two!'

(**42** 5) indicate that Harry finally accepts the situation apparently without gritting his teeth. Sheila, too, acknowledges that she and Harry are 'beaten fair and square' (**42** 6).

8. *Why are Harry and Sheila more relaxed together after Jim and Jane have gone away?*
They feel relieved. The stress of competitions is now over. Their opponents have gone. Now they can relax. There is no need to strain every nerve any longer and to try to get the better of their opponents. Harry and Sheila are no longer under terrible pressure. They can talk freely and openly about what has happened.

9. *How do Harry and Sheila describe their opponents? (**42** 20–**43** 24)*
Jim and Jane are described as the incarnation of the ideal couple. Jim is brilliant and has a good job with wonderful prospects. Jane is unusually beautiful, shiny, smooth, a lovely girl, whose stylish and attractive appearance is admired by everybody.

They make a very handsome, happy and well-adjusted couple. They are perfect tennis players and just 'mad about each other' (**42** 31). Apparently their relationship is without any blemish except perhaps for the fact that 'they *know* it' (**43** 3).

In their conversation, however, Harry and Sheila realize that the couple's perfection and beauty is somehow marred. Jane must spend a lot of time and money to keep up her 'glossy look' (**43** 4–5). Jim seems to be under severe strain because he is forced to 'outguess everyone else' and to always keep 'one jump ahead' (**43** 13). His brain seems almost to be 'ticking away' (**43** 9–10). Obviously both Jim and Jane are in a permanent state of anxiety, tension or exhaustion caused by competition. They are the victims of constant demand on their physical and mental strength, resources and abilities. Somehow they are compelled to be always 'on the go' or 'on the ball'.

Suggestions for the blackboard: see p 108.

10. *Describe Harry and Sheila's realization at the end.*
Harry and Sheila finally come to terms with the facts as they are ('Well, let's face it'; **43** 11). Their opponents, Jim and Jane, are entirely different from them. Harry and Sheila realize that they are no match for Jim and Jane. They would have to take up intensive tennis training (**42** 21), or even bridge (**42** 25), if they really wanted to imitate that attractive, successful, well-adjusted couple.

Harry realizes that he wouldn't be able to keep up a competitive lifestyle like Jim, and Sheila realizes that he would therefore not make the right partner for Jane. She senses that Harry would never get far with Jane, and that she would have no need to be jealous of her (**42** 28–29). Sheila gets the feeling of pressure (**43** 9) whenever she thinks of Jim.

JIM
brainy
brilliant
clever
successful
bright
smart
(**43** 6–8/12)

→ **IDEAL COUPLE** ←
(**42** 21–22/31; **43** 1)
happy
well-adjusted
'mad about each other'
handsome

JANE
beautiful
lovely
unusual
shiny
attractive
stylish
glossy look
(**42** 32; **43** 2/5)

BUT

strain of competition
- 'strain of always keeping one jump ahead' (**43** 12)
- 'trying to outguess everyone else' (**43** 13)
- 'his brain's ticking away' (**43** 9)

strain of keeping up beauty
- 'all the time she must spend – to say nothing of money – keeping up that glossy look' (**43** 4–5)

Blackboard suggestions for question 9 on p 107.

In the end, both Harry and Sheila realize that 'there's more to life than that' (**43** 22–23) and that life without the strains of competitiveness can also be rewarding. That's why Sheila turns to look at Harry (**43** 24). Apparently they love each other. The audience (the reader) gradually comes to the conclusion that *they* might be the *real* winners of the match because of this realization.

On the other hand, their realization might also be interpreted as a (very human) 'sour grapes' attitude to what they would very much like to have – but know they can never attain. They would lose face (towards each other – and themselves personally) if they admitted the extent of their admiration of the other two. The wiser – and the only – course is to save themselves from self-contempt by taking up the attitude that there are other things in life, too.

Unit 4: Further Structural and Thematic Aspects of the Play

1. *What is the 'message' of the play?*
Suggested answers:
- *Score* is a play about competition, about winning and losing.
- *Score* is a play about appearance and reality. Jim and Jane, a perfect couple, keep up appearances successfully. They are the winners. Harry and Sheila, on the other hand, are the losers. But the audience can easily imagine what might happen if Jim and Jane lost one day.
- *Score* is a play about stress and tension. The fact that Harry and Sheila's self-imposed goal is unattainable causes mental and physical stress and distress. The play reveals various examples of how people can behave when they are under stress and how their relationship can be strained.
- *Score* is a play about the relativity of success. Who's the winner in the end?
- *Score* shows how people can make fools of themselves in a competitive situation and how easily they can lose control of themselves. *Score* is a criticism of today's world of competitiveness (the 'rat race' in today's society).
- *Score* shows that a man who is at a disadvantage in a competitive situation is much more prone to lose control than a woman. (This could also be a point for discussion).

2. *How is the audience drawn into the play?*
The audience must cooperate in that they must complete the imaginary dialogues. The strange thing is that the audience is on 'our' side (– Jim and Jane's side; cf. **36** 9). Thus each member of the audience is more or less forced to identify him-/herself with Jim or Jane, who finally win. To a certain extent the audience is enabled and allowed to develop a sense of superiority. It is 'our' (= Jim and Jane's) side that wins.

3. *Try and draw a diagram of the structure of the plot.*
Suggestions: see overleaf.

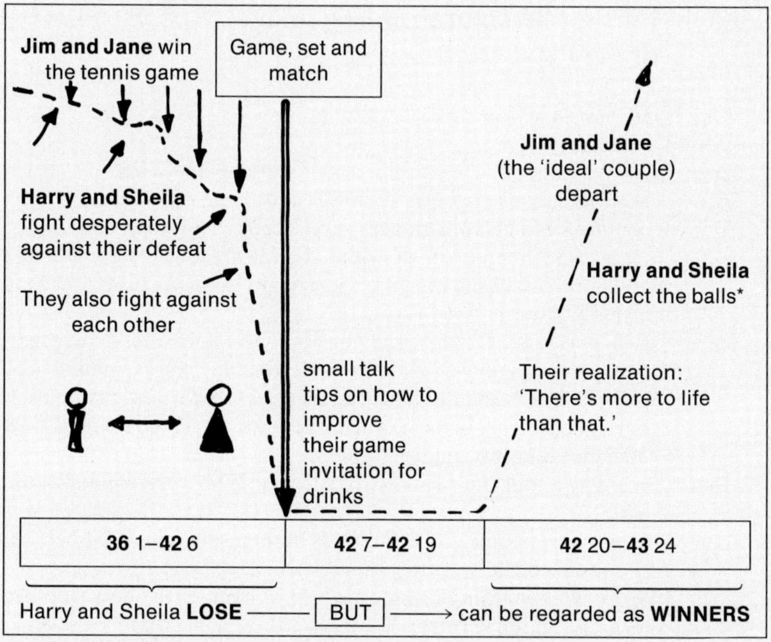

* Almost as though Jim and Jane deliberately leave them to do this – the only thing they can be relied on to do properly.

Additional activities

The following poem can be discussed and interpreted:

'40	**–**	**Love'**
middle		aged
couple		playing
ten		nis
when		the
game		ends
and		they
go		home
the		net
will		still
be		be
tween		them

From *After the Merrymaking* by Roger McGough, London: Jonathan Cape, 1971.

Aspects for discussion:
- ambiguity of title
- love at the age of forty (a kind of stock-taking of a middle-aged couple)
- net = the dividing wall (of relationship)
- eyes are forced to read to and fro (as in a tennis game)
- when quoting the poem you are forced to speak in a clipped way that imitates the sound of the tennis ball
- form (concrete poetry)

Students like writing poetry themselves. The following examples, written by students of the Kepler-Gymnasium in Tübingen, are to encourage the teacher as well as the students to write little poems like these:

15 – LOVE

love – is
like – a
ten – nis
game – with
out – a
n~~e~~t

TENNIS

When – playing
tennis
you – can
cometogether
or – be
co – me
fierce – opponents

APPEARANCE AND REALITY

push – ups
fit – ness
life – style
bo – dy
build – ing
beau – ty
glossy – look
T I M E
col – lapse

Roy Minton

Bovver

Characters:

VIC

TERRY

PAUL

Scene:

A ground-floor bedsitter. It is shabbily furnished, the main furniture being two single beds, wardrobe, chest of drawers and two battered leather easy chairs. A small wooden upright chair is beside one of the beds. In one corner, a sink and gas ring. Two cheap, worn suitcases are stacked on top of the wardrobe. No effort has been made to dress the room, apart from several nude pin-ups above one bed, a German helmet and flag on the wall beside the other, together with a large picture of Hitler.

TERRY *and* VIC *are seated –* TERRY *on the edge of a bed,* VIC *in an easy chair.* TERRY *is 17 or 18 years old, with hair cropped to skinhead order; he wears regulation braces and boots.* VIC *is in his early thirties: stocky, broad-shouldered, with large hands. They are both eating chips from paper wrappers and are completely immersed in this function. The muffled sound of a radio can be heard emanating from a pile of bedding and carpets in the centre of the room.*

1	bovver ['bɒvə]	dialect pronunciation of *bother* = trouble
7	a bedsitter [ˌ–'––]	a room used for both living and sleeping in
	shabby	old and worn
8	battered ['bætəd]	old and worn
10	**a sink**	a basin with a water tap
	a gas ring	a small gas cooker
	to stack things	to pile things up, to put one thing on top of the other
12	a nude pin-up [nju:d]	a poster of a naked girl
15	to crop s.th.	to cut s.th. very short
16	regulation	*here:* the typical kind of
	braces ['breɪsɪz]	straps holding trousers up *(Hosenträger)*
	stocky	short and strong; solid in appearance
18	immersed [ɪ'mɜ:sd]	absorbed
	muffled	faint
19	to emanate from ['eməneɪt]	to come from

TERRY *finishes his chips, screws up the paper and throws it in the wardrobe. He picks up two brooms and crosses to* VIC. VIC *ignores him.* TERRY *stands, waiting until* VIC *has eaten his chips and screwed up the paper wrapping. He hands* VIC *a broom and tosses the paper into the wardrobe.* VIC *sucks his teeth, smacks his lips and stands.*

They begin stamping up and down the room, banging the broom handles on the floor and crashing their boots as noisily as possible. This continues for several seconds until they hear a door slam downstairs.

They immediately dash to hide the brooms. VIC *carries the bedding to a bed and spreads it tidily.* TERRY *lifts up a floorboard and retrieves a radio playing at full volume. He switches off the radio and hides it, then replaces the floorboard. They are spreading the tatty carpeting on the floor when there is a knock at the door.* TERRY *looks at the door and sniggers.* VIC *glares and* TERRY *covers his mouth with his palm.* VIC *puts a finger to his lips and calls towards the door.*

VIC: One moment.

(TERRY *sniggers behind his palm.* VIC *checks that the room is in order. He reverses the picture of Hitler. Queen Elizabeth is on the reverse side. He checks that the room is in order. He crosses to open the door. An embarrassed* PAUL *is standing outside. He is a second-year student, an ordinary, gentle young man, slim, with hair longish but not overdone. He wears spectacles.)*

VIC: Ah, monsieur …

PAUL: Sorry to disturb you but –

VIC: Come in, come in, monsieur. Be my guest.

PAUL: Well, I don't really have time. Just wanted to say, ask –

VIC: Ahh, you'd insult us, effendi? It may be humble but … come in. Do.

(He pulls PAUL *inside and closes the door.)*

VIC: Sit down.

PAUL: No, I won't stay.

2	**a broom**	*Besen*
4	to toss	to throw (a light object)
9	**to dash**	to run quickly
10	to retrieve s.th. [rɪ'tri:v]	to get s.th. back from the place where you left it
12	tatty	dirty, shabby
13	to snigger	to laugh in a disrespectful way
14	to glare [gleə]	to look at s.o. or s.th. angrily
	the palm (of the hand) [ɑ:]	the inner surface of the hand
18	**to reverse s.th.** [rɪ'vɜ:s]	to turn s.th. the other way round
27	effendi [ɪ'fendɪ]	*Turkish:* Sir, master

VIC *(smiling but threatening)*: Sit down, squire.

PAUL: Yes, well, for a moment.

(He crosses towards an easy chair but TERRY *jumps in and sits in it.* VIC *fetches the upright chair and places it in the centre of the room.)*

VIC: Sit there, sahib.

PAUL: Shouldn't really.

VIC: Oh, I should. (PAUL *sits.*) I'd offer you Scotch, but as you can see, the decanter's empty and there's no one to nip down to the off-licence. Butler's day off. Terrible problems with staff these days. Yes, absolutely bloody awful. Don't you find?

PAUL: Look, Vic …

VIC: Pardon?

PAUL: Your name is Vic, isn't it?

VIC: Ah, now hang on, hang on. I don't think we've been introduced, have we, Terry? (TERRY *stares coldly at* PAUL.) No. See.

PAUL: I just thought, I'd heard –

VIC: Well, I'm a stickler for procedure, yes, definite proclivity for the formalities of life, as you might comprehend if you knew me, er shall we say, more intimately. Rather partial to formality.

PAUL: I'm, er, I'm Paul. I live downstairs.

VIC: I'm well aware of that, señor. Yes, indeed.

(Pause.)

PAUL *(offering his hand)*: Paul. Paul Watson.

VIC *(ignores the handshake and bows)*: Mister Owen. And this is Mister Breedon. Mister Terry Breedon.

1	squire *(dialectal)* ['skwaɪə]	a form of address among men (used only to s.o. of higher social class)
5	sahib [sɑ:b]	used in India in former times as a title of respect for a European man
8	a decanter [dɪ'kæntə]	a container for holding alcoholic drinks
	to nip down *(coll.)*	to go down
	an off-licence	a shop which sells alcoholic drinks
14	Hang on *(coll.)*	Wait a bit.
17	a stickler for procedure ['stɪklə, prə'si:dʒə]	a person who insist on correct behaviour
	a proclivity for s.th. *(lit.)* [prə'klɪvɪtɪ]	a liking for or tendency towards s.th.
18	to comprehend [ˌkɒmprɪ'hend]	to understand
19	to be partial to s.th. ['pɑ:ʃəl]	to have a strong liking for s.th.

PAUL: Hello.

(TERRY *simply stares at him.)*

VIC: Mister Breedon and I are just good friends. Yes. He's what you might call my protégé, and yet in a sense we're brothers. Not that we shared the same womb, no, just the common-or-garden blood variety. A small slit in the wrist, press together and the blood mingles, little pain attached to it – so we have some bond, something more than mere acquaintance. You know the sort of thing I mean. Blood brothers, yes. And there's also the more intimate business of our similar tattoos, eagles, on our chests, in flight – but that's not intended for public exposure. No. Hardly call us exhibitionists. Don't go for the flashing bit. Right, what can I do for you?

PAUL: Well, it was the noise –

VIC: That chair comfortable?

PAUL: What?

VIC: COMFY, ARE YOU?

PAUL: Yes, yes thanks.

VIC: Don't want you wriggling a sore bum on that wooden seat. Fancy a lie-down? Two beds there, empty, doing nothing.

PAUL: This is fine.

VIC *(effusive)*: You're welcome.

PAUL: No, fine ...

VIC: Ah, good. Just don't want any aspersions cast on the quality of our hospitality.

4	protégé ['prɒtɪʒeɪ]	a person who is guided and helped by s.o. of influence or power
5	**womb** [wu:m]	*Mutterleib*
	common-or-garden	ordinary, usual
	variety [və'raɪətɪ]	*here:* type, sort
	a slit	a cut
6	**to mingle** ['mɪŋgl]	to mix
9	**a tattoo** [tə'tu:]	*Tätowierung*
	an eagle ['i:gl]	*Adler*
10	**exposure** [ɪk'spəʊʒə]	display, exhibition
11	Don't go for the flashing bit. *(sl.)*	We aren't keen on behaving like exhibionists.
17	to wriggle ['rɪgl]	to move quickly from side to side; *here:* to get by wriggling
	sore [sɔ:]	painful, aching
	bum *(sl.)* [bʌm]	the part of the body on which a person sits
20	effusive [ɪ'fju:sɪv]	showing (too) much feeling
22	to cast aspersions on s.th. [kɑ:st, ə'spɜ:ʃənz] *(lit.)*	to raise doubts about s.th., to make damaging remarks about s.th.

PAUL: It was the noise.

VIC: Eh?

PAUL: I wanted to speak to you about the noise.

VIC: My dear Terry, what is the gentleman talking about?

PAUL: Don't like to complain, you understand. I wouldn't unless ... but the radio blaring away, seemed to come from your floor straight through my ceiling. I was trying to work, you see, and all the stamping and banging, well, I know we give and take, but if you could, just a little quieter, I do a lot of work in my room.

TERRY: Work? Student's work!?

PAUL: Studying. It's the concentration ...

VIC: Do I hear straight? Am I to understand that you are making allegations against me and my blood brother, Mister Terry Breedon? Radio, in this room? There's been some mistake, surely.

PAUL: If you wouldn't mind, the volume down, just a little.

VIC: Can you see a radio? Here?

PAUL: Well, not just now.

VIC: Can you? No. Or a licence? Eh? Perhaps you'd like to scratch around for a licence? Well go ahead, sir, go ahead, take the place apart, but I can assure you, you won't find a scrap of evidence here. Not a crystal.

PAUL: Look, have your joke, only –

VIC: Not a scrap. You from the fuzz?

PAUL: What?

VIC: Any connection with Lilly Law?

PAUL: I don't ...

VIC: Police?

PAUL: Oh. No, of course not.

VIC: Course not? Why course? Somebody's connected with 'em, aren't they? We presume they've all got parents – disappointed with their

6	**to blare** [bleə]	to produce loud and unpleasant sounds
12	to make allegations against s.o. [ælɪ'geɪʃənz]	to accuse s.o. of s.th. without having any proof
15	**volume** ['vɒlju:m]	strength of sound (radio, TV)
18	to scratch around for s.th. *(coll.)*	to look for s.th. here and there
20	a scrap	a bit, a small piece
22	the fuzz *(sl.)* [fʌz]	the police
24	Lilly Law *(sl.)*	the police

offspring, yes, I'll grant you that – but connected nonetheless. Somebody cops for 'em.

PAUL: Nothing to do with me.

VIC: So we can trust you?

PAUL: Trust me?

VIC: We've nothing to hide, you know. Have we, Terry? No, clean as a whistle. So any further pursuit with your investigation will prove futile, I'm afraid. No good setting your hush puppies loose in here. Sorry I can't offer you a drink, inspector.

PAUL *(stands)*: Look, I haven't time to listen to you rambling on, so if you'll kindly keep the noise down I'll be grateful.

*(*VIC *blocks his path to the door.* TERRY *crosses to lean on the door. Pause.* VIC *stares at* PAUL *and carefully rolls up his shirtsleeves an extra turn.)*

VIC *(quietly)*: That was an untimely outburst. Terry didn't like that. He doesn't like hospitality thrown back in his face. Bit of a stickler for the social graces. I should have mentioned that before.

PAUL: May I leave?

VIC *(standing menacingly in front of him)*: Leave? So soon?

TERRY: Sit down!

PAUL: Who do you think you're –

VIC: Ohh, steady, steady, Mister – what did you say your name was?

PAUL: WATSON.

VIC: Ah, yes. Easy, Mister Watson. When Terry actually speaks it's time to watch your Ps and Qs.

PAUL: I'll watch what I think fit!

TERRY: Down!

PAUL *(a little frightened)*: Now, look ...

1	offspring ['ɒfsprɪŋ]	a child or children of a particular person
2	to cop for *(sl.)*	to be responsible for
7	pursuit *(lit.)* [pə'sju:t]	*here:* continuation
	investigation [ɪnˌvestɪ'geɪʃn]	examination
	futile ['fju:taɪl]	useless
8	hush puppies [hʌʃ'pʌpɪz] *(sl.)*	police dogs
10	to ramble ['ræmbl]	to talk without keeping to the subject
16	the social graces ['greɪsɪz]	polite manners
18	**menacing** ['menəsɪŋ]	threatening
24	to watch one's Ps and Qs	to be very careful to use suitable language
25	to think fit	to consider s.th. right or suitable

VIC *(shouts)*: Heel!

PAUL: Pardon?

VIC: Heel! Heel, Rover!

(PAUL *doesn't know what to do.* VIC *prods him in the chest and he sits in the upright chair.)*

Now then, Mister … whatever you are. Do I understand that you're making a complaint of noise emanating from this apartment?

PAUL: No, not a –

VIC: Because, Mister Whatsit, if that is so, we shall have to look into the matter.

PAUL: Look, why don't we just forget it?

VIC: Ah, now then, that's not on, not on at all. We can't have blemishes plastered all over our character at the drop of a hat, then just forget it. Hardly be democratic, would it?

PAUL: I'm not accusing anybody.

VIC: Not to mention other aspects of the case.

PAUL: What case?

VIC: I think I ought to put you in the picture before you go dashing off for Edgar Lustgarten, eh?

(PAUL *stares at the floor, resigned and confused.)*

You see, Mister Breedon and I have just dined out. Nothing extravagant or foreign, mind you, just a quiet tête-à-tête in the most discreet corner of a well-established English restaurant up West. Oysters weren't up to scratch, but the rest of the meal first-class. Yes, top hole. A fair nosh. A walk through the park, give the digestive organs a chance to get into gear, a taxi to the front door and into our apartment just in time to hear you

1	Heel! [hi:l]	command given to a dog to walk close behind its master
3	Rover ['rəʊvə]	a common dog's name
4	to prod s.o.	to push or press s.o. with a finger or a pointed object
7	**a complaint** [kəm'pleɪnt]	a statement of dissatisfaction
12	That's not on. *(coll.)*	You can't do that; that's not possible.
	a blemish ['blemɪʃ]	a stain, a defect
13	at the drop of a hat	at once, suddenly
19	Edgar Lustgarten ['edgə'lʌstgɑ:tn]	TV and radio journalist who did programmes on famous criminal cases, legal proceedings, etc.
22	mind you	however
23	an oyster ['ɔɪstə]	*Auster*
	up to scratch *(coll.)*	up to standard, statisfactory
24	top hole *(sl.)*	first class
	a fair nosh *(sl.)*	a good meal
25	**digestive** [daɪ'dʒestɪv]	helping in the digestion *(Verdauung)* of food

slam – slam – your door and pound up here to lodge this incredible complaint.

PAUL *(half moans, halfs sighs)*: Ohh …

VIC: You tired?

PAUL: No. I just want to go.

VIC: Good. So there was hardly time for us to … stamp, was it? And as for the radio … well, to put it in a nutshell, we haven't got one. So what do we make of that, eh?

PAUL: You know damned well what was going on!

VIC: Oh, language, please, please. Unless … Terry, a distressing thought occurs to me. Burglars. Yes. Suppose Mister Whatsit heard burglars and, being a good neighbour, a responsible member of society, came up here to investigate on our behalf. Do you think we've had burglars? Is that possible? Here, Terry, have a butchers. Check if any property's been misappropriated.

*(*TERRY *crosses to stand behind* PAUL.*)*

That is the word, I believe. Though you'd know better, being an intellectual, and I'll gladly bend to your superior knowledge if you care to improve from your immeasurable vocabulary. No? Right. Misappropriated. I should be most upset if the family heirlooms were nicked. Indeed.

(He looks around the room.)

No, everything here. Your examination prove O.K., Terry? Good. Yes, everything in order. All heirlooms and valuables intact? Good. Fine. So. I don't know what to make of your accusation.

PAUL: Not accusation!

VIC: No? Oh. Mmm.

(Pause.)

You having psychiatric treatment, are you?

*(*PAUL *sighs, exasperated.)*

1	to lodge a complaint [lɒdʒ]	to make a formal complaint
7	to put it in a nutshell *(coll.)*	briefly speaking, in short
10	distressing [dɪ'stresɪŋ]	upsetting, saddening
14	to have a butchers *(sl.)* ['bʊtʃəz]	to have a look
15	to misappropriate s.th. [ˌmɪsə'prəʊprɪeɪt]	*here:* to steal s.th.
20	an heirloom ['eəlu:m]	a valuable object handed down in a family for several generations
	to nick s.th. *(sl.)*	to steal s.th.
29	**exasperated** [ɪg'zæspəreɪtɪd]	extremely annoyed and angry

TERRY: Answer!

*(*PAUL *starts to turn to* TERRY, *but* VIC *is quickly on to him.)*

VIC: Hallucinations? History of mental disorder in the family? Any of your close relatives been certified?

PAUL: I want to go.

VIC: This may turn out to be a bother. One for the flying doctor. Like an aspirin? Eh?

TERRY: Answer!

PAUL: No.

TERRY: No, what?!

PAUL: Thanks.

VIC: I did warn you, squire, Mister Breedon's most particular, a dab hand at good manners. Oh yes. You'd be well advised to tread carefully in that direction. Mmm …

TERRY: Apologize.

*(*PAUL *does not move.)*

Let's bleeding give it him.

VIC: Gently, blood brother. I'm sure our guest will do the honourable thing.

TERRY: Apologize.

*(*PAUL *looks at* VIC *for guidance, points a finger back at* TERRY. VIC *smiles and nods.)*

PAUL: Sorry.

VIC *(whispers confidentially)*: Mister Breedon.

PAUL: Mister Breedon.

VIC: Happy, Terry?

(No response. TERRY *stares at the back of* PAUL*'s head.)*

Good. Of course, mental illness is nothing to be ashamed of these days, Mister … Whatsit … that is your name, isn't it? Eh?!

PAUL: Watson.

4	to certify s.o. ['sɜ:tɪfaɪ]	to declare s.o. officially mad
12	a dab hand at s.th. *(coll.)*	a person who is very good at s.th.; an expert
17	bleeding *(sl.)*	swear word used for emphasis (as an adjective or adverb)
24	confidential [ˌkɒnfɪ'denʃəl]	private, intimate

VIC: Ah, yes. Forgetful of me. Perhaps if I call you Doctor that'll be nearer the point and avoid confusion. Doctor Watson – Sherlock's fiancé. Yes. As I was saying, Doctor, sickness in the head's as common as the cold. Everybody's at it. A touch of the headaches, two penn'orth of shoplifting and it's six months at the funny farm, munching tranquillisers breakfast, dinner and tea – day after day on the couch, revealing your innermost privacy to some nosey git in a white coat. Not everybody's cup of tea by any means, but there's plenty of 'em at it. Dossing and noshing on the National Health. Scavengers, the most of 'em. Yes, there's none of the old stigma attached to a spell in the bighouse. Sort of social prerequisite in certain areas. Unless you've copped for the regulation nervous breakdowns, you're not quite 'In'. Got to be twitching about in the latter stages of epilepsy, stammering self-indulgent neuroses through your olive-dropped cocktail before you're taken seriously these days ... that's what I find, anyway. Not a chance of setting foot on Hampstead Heath unless you're nipping from tree to tree clutching a tin of pills, or

2	Sherlock	allusion to the detective stories about Sherlock Holmes and Dr. Watson by Sir Arthur Conan Doyle
	fiancé [fɪ'ɑ:nseɪ]	man to whom a woman is engaged to be married
4	a penn'orth ['penəθ] *(coll.)*	a pennyworth ['penɪwəθ] (as much as can be bought for a penny); a little
5	a funny farm *(sl.)*	a mental hospital
	to munch	to eat or chew
	a tranquillizer	a drug to calm one down
7	nosey ['nəʊzɪ] *(coll.)*	interested in things that do not concern one; inquisitive
	a git *(sl.)* [gɪt]	a contemptible person, a fool
	(not) to be s.o.'s cup of tea *(coll.)*	(not) to please s.o.
8	to doss *(sl.)*	to sleep, especially not on a proper bed
	to nosh *(sl.)*	to eat
9	a scavenger ['skævɪndʒə]	a person who searches for food among waste
10	**a spell**	a period of time
	a bighouse *(sl.)*	a prison
	a prerequisite [pri:'rekwɪzɪt]	s.th. that is necessary before s.th. else can be done or happen; a condition
11	to cop for *(sl.)*	*here:* to have, to suffer
12	to twitch	to make sudden uncontrolled movements
13	epilepsy ['– – – –]	
	self-indulgent ['selfɪnˌdʌldʒənt]	selfish; giving oneself things that one enjoys
15	Hampstead Heath ['hæmpstɪd 'hi:θ]	popular recreation area in North London

else a fully-fledged piss artist. No, the better areas aren't what they were. So you think you're schizophrenic?

PAUL *(gestures helplessly with his hands before getting his words out):* I … I am just a student, second-year, living in the basement immediately below you. I am trying to work, but my concentration is continually broken by … by a barrage … assaults from this room at all hours of the day and night. I have not complained before, but it is affecting my work. I'm losing sleep.

TERRY *(with disgust)*: Student!

PAUL: I only ask that you're a little more considerate, that's all.

VIC: Losing sleep. Eh?

PAUL: Yes.

VIC: Well now, aren't we all?

PAUL: My work's deteriorating.

VIC: I see.

(Pause.)

PAUL: So if –

TERRY: Parties!

VIC: Pardon, blood brother?

TERRY: Parties.

VIC: Ah. We are coming to that. Yes. A sensitive point. Indeed. Hardly let this gathering pass without mentioning your parties, could we, Doctor?

PAUL: If you two want to discuss your social engagements, I'll get back to my room.

TERRY: Heel!

PAUL *(startled)*: What?

VIC *(quietly; he winks at* PAUL*):* Heel!

PAUL: Please.

1	fully-fledged [fledʒd]	fully grown; experienced
	a piss artist *(sl.)*	a person who drinks heavily and often gets drunk
2	schizophrenic [ˌskɪtsəʊ'frenɪk]	
6	a barrage ['bærɑ:ʒ]	continuous 'gunfire'
	an assault [ə'sɔ:lt]	a sudden violent attack
10	**considerate** [kən'sɪdərət]	thoughtful of the needs of others
14	to deteriorate [dɪ'tɪərɪəreɪt]	to become worse
21	**sensitive** ['– – –]	*here:* problematic, to be treated with tact
27	**startled**	surprised
28	**to wink**	to close one eye briefly, especially as a private signal

VIC: See how it is, Doc? We don't spend our leisure time in here completely undisturbed.

PAUL: What are you talking about?

VIC *(suddenly moves in; presses his face close to* PAUL'S *and shouts):* Parties! Orgies! All-night bloody rave-ups in your pornographic basement room!

PAUL: Don't shout at me!

TERRY: Heel!

PAUL: Shut up!

TERRY *(closing in)*: Eh?

PAUL: Don't talk to me like that, yobbo!

(Pause. TERRY *fetches a bicycle chain and crosses to stand over* PAUL, *the chain dangling from his hand.* VIC *draws in breath through his pursed lips and expels it, shaking his head.)*

VIC: You really do go over the top, Doctor. Push your luck something rotten, don't you?

TERRY: Fancies his chance, don't he?

VIC: I mean, I like spirit, yes, but in moderation, please. Where would any of us be without discipline? Goodness me, I mean to say, various gentlemen in a variety of institutions have been to great pains to convince me of the necessity of discipline, both self-imposed and the other. Were quite insistent, *and* government-backed. So I do speak with some authority.

TERRY: Let me have him, Vic.

PAUL: You'd better tell your friend to put his toy away.

TERRY: Watch it, prat!

PAUL: Don't you dare touch me.

VIC *(pleasantly)*: Why not, Doctor?

(Pause.)

PAUL: I'm non-violent.

VIC: Pacifist, are we?

PAUL: Yes. Not that it's any of your business.

5	a rave-up *(sl.)* ['reɪvˌʌp]	a (lively) party
10	a yobbo *(sl.)* ['jɒbəʊ]	a rough vulgar young man; a hooligan
12	**to dangle** ['dæŋgl]	to hang or swing loosely
	to purse one's lips [pɜːs]	to bring one's lips together in little folds
13	to expel s.th. [ɪk'spel]	to push s.th. out
14	to go over the top	to overdo s.th.
	to push one's luck	to take a risk; to go too far
	something rotten *(sl.)*	a bit too much; terribly
17	spirit	*here:* courage
24	a prat *(sl.)*	a worthless, stupid person; a fool

TERRY: Four-eyed git!

VIC: Ah, now, Terry, easy. The poor Doctor's got his head in the books. Strains his eyes.

TERRY *(showing the chain)*: Wants this straining round his head.

PAUL: Tell him to put it away.

VIC: Yes, what I was saying, Doc – you see, we've put up with all your hanky-panky downstairs with never so much as a murmur, just thought to ourselves – no, do not go down those steps and kick the shit out of him. Live and let live, that's been our motto, for want of a better word – but you, the first sign of intrusion, a burglar on the premises, clomping about with a full-blast transistor in his handbag, and you're galloping up here like a busload of fuzz, dragging us up the Old Bailey. As though it's our fault. Now I wouldn't call that good neighbours. Hardly togetherness, is it? After all we have had to stand. Losing sleep and gritting our understanding teeth while you and your mates are up to your bag of tricks down there, all hours!

PAUL: I'm warning you –

VIC: Three in the morning! At it till three in the morning!

PAUL: I've never disturbed you. I'm careful about noise.

TERRY: You calling us a liar?

PAUL *(deliberately)*: There has been no excessive noise from my room.

VIC: What about the party?

PAUL: What party? When?

VIC: Two bloody weeks ago – when!

PAUL: Oh.

VIC: To name but one, eh, Terry?

TERRY: I nearly had a breakdown. Bloody house full of students.

VIC: It was most unpleasant.

PAUL: That was my birthday.

VIC: Call it what you will, Doc, it had my blood brother on the verge of

1	four-eyed *(sl.)*	wearing glasses
3	**to strain**	to stretch or pull tight; to weaken by overuse
6	to put up with s.th. *(coll.)*	to tolerate s.th.
7	hanky-panky [ˌ– –'– –]	doubtful (esp. sexual) behaviour
10	**intrusion** [ɪn'tru:ʒn]	disturbance of privacy
	the premises ['premɪsɪz]	the house (with its surrounding land)
	to clomp (*or* clump)	to walk with heavy steps
12	the Old Bailey	the chief criminal court in London
14	**to grit one's teeth**	to press one's teeth tightly together
15	your mates *(coll.)*	your friends
30	**on the verge of** [vɜ:dʒ]	very near to

tears. And nervous ... I had to lay the boot in to sedate him. Bag of shakes, he was. Most unpleasant.

PAUL: I came up, came up to let you know I was having that party. Knocked on your door, was going to ask you down for a drink. You didn't answer. I was sure you were in, but you didn't answer.

VIC: No? Well, could have been the butler's day off.

PAUL: It was my birthday. I came up to ask if you'd mind us playing records late, on that one occasion. If you check with the person living in the next room he'll tell you. I spoke to him, he said he didn't mind. If you choose not to answer your door that's your affair, but *I*, at least, did behave responsibly.

VIC *(thoughtfully)*: Mmmm ...

TERRY: Up all bleeding night, I was.

VIC: No doubt about that.

TERRY: Raving, weren't they? Bleeding hooligans. And I've not forgot you calling me a yobbo, student!

PAUL: Just ... forget it.

TERRY: Oh yes.

VIC: Mmm, a most unfortunate slip of the tongue. And Mister Breedon has an astoundingly retentive memory. You'd be amazed at the things that stick in his head, he's a continuous surprise to me. Comes out with some right pearlers. You had a load of birds down there, did you?

PAUL: Pardon?

TERRY *(to* VIC*)*: He knows!

VIC: Down your rave-up. We heard the giggles, in fact if the butler had been here we'd have got him to switch on the tape recorder, could have played the evidence back to you – but we did do just a spot of earwigging. Quite an orgy down there, eh?

PAUL: No.

VIC: Plenty of birds, though, weren't there?

PAUL: There were –

1	to lay the boot in *(sl.)*	to kick s.o. hard; to act with determination
	to sedate s.o. [sɪ'deɪt]	to calm s.o. down
2	shakes [ʃeɪks]	nervous shaking of the body
15	**to rave** [reɪv]	to behave loudly and wildly; to shout
20	astounding [ə'staʊndɪŋ]	amazing, astonishing
	retentive [rɪ'tentɪv]	able to keep things in mind
22	a pearler *(sl.)*	something outstandingly good
	a bird *(sl.)*	a girl
25	a giggle ['gɪgl]	a silly or nervous laugh
27	earwigging ['ɪəwɪgɪŋ] *(sl.)*	listening to s.th. that does not concern one

VIC: We heard! Right above you, aren't we? Can't miss. Weren't singing bloody hymns, were we? All had their clothes on, did they? Eh? What kind of filth was going on in the same house I have to live in? Eh?

PAUL: There was nothing like that.

VIC: Like what? Like what? You seem to be remarkably well informed on the subject of pornography.

PAUL: It was my birthday party. Some friends and a few chicks, that's all.

VIC: Chicks?

PAUL: Yes, friends.

VIC: Chicks?! Chicks?! Why don't you talk proper? They're birds. That's what they're called – birds. What are they?

PAUL: Girls.

VIC: Birds!

PAUL: Birds.

TERRY: Crumpet! Crumpet!

PAUL: Crumpet.

VIC: Better.

PAUL: Please ... *(Pause.)* May I go?

VIC: So you weren't all naked down there? Weren't prancing and groping, starkers?

PAUL: No.

VIC: Then what the bloody hell's the matter with you? What's wrong? Can't manage it, eh? Bent, are you? Is that it? Bent? Nine-bob note, are we? Well, I'll tell you something, Doctor, we don't take kindly to that sort of thing. Do we, Terry? Don't fancy the homos.

TERRY: Perverts!

VIC: No, don't go down with us at all. I mean, Terry here does his fair

3	**filth** [fɪlθ]	dirt
7	a chick [tʃɪk] *(sl.)*	a girl
15	crumpet *(sl.)* ['krʌmpɪt]	collective term for women as sexual objects *(very rude!)*
19	to prance [prɑ:ns]	to move quickly with a dancing step
	to grope *(sl.)* [grəʊp]	to (try to) touch s.o.'s body so as to get sexual pleasure
20	starkers *(sl.)* ['stɑ:kəz]	stark (totally) naked
23	bent *(sl.)*	homosexual
	a nine-bob note *(sl.)*	a nine-shilling note (which didn't exist)
27	to go down with s.o. *(sl.)*	to please s.o.; to be popular with s.o.

whack. Does his best. Puts in his stint of Paki-bashing regular as clockwork, yes. Somebody's got to. Country's going to the dogs – be falling in the bloody seas soon, tipping off the cliffs. Flaming country's chock full of 'em. Jews, Irish, Pakis, Jocks, Poles – what's happening to the English, I ask myself. Where's the Empire? This is anthropology gone mad. Mind you, the government's getting things sorted out – not like that Labour lot when they were in. Let 'em all come, that was their motto; didn't have to live with 'em, did they? No. All up to blokes like us, innit. Public spirited, give 'em the hint, all these bleeding wogs. Put the boot about, yes. Yes. That's one thing ... But if there's something that really drives him – and me – potty, it's your bleeding queers. Gives 'em a bashing, Terry does. Yes. Say 'thank you' to Mister Breedon. Government-backed, we are now. Got old Enoch behind us. Say 'thank you' for saving England.

PAUL *(stands determinedly)*: I've had enough of this, I'm going.

*(*VIC *and* TERRY *move in close.)*

VIC: Are we?

PAUL: There'll be trouble.

TERRY: Yes.

PAUL: So, if you two don't mind ...

VIC: Got any hobbies, have you?

PAUL: Look ...!

VIC: Hobbies, I said! *(Pause, quietly:)* Hobbies, squire. *(Pause.)*

PAUL: Ornithology.

VIC: Oh, I say. Hear that, blood brother? Ornithology.

TERRY: Prat.

1	to do one's whack *(sl.)* [wæk]	to do one's share, to do one's part
	Puts in his stint of ...	He does his share of ...
	Paki-bashing *(sl.)*	racially motivated attacks on the Pakistanis, esp. by white skinhead youths
3	chock full	crowded; completely full
4	Jocks *(sl.)*	Scots
6	to get things sorted out	to solve the problems
8	a bloke *(sl.)* [bləuk]	a man
	innit	isn't it
	public spirited	willing to act in the public interest
9	a wog *(sl.)* [wɒg]	any non-white, esp. an Indian
11	potty *(sl.)* ['pɒtɪ]	crazy
	a queer *(sl.)* [kwɪə]	a homosexual
13	Enoch Powell ['i:nɒk 'paʊəl]	a British politician extremely opposed to Commonwealth immigration into Britain
23	ornithology [ˌɔ:nɪ'θɒlədʒɪ]	the scientific study of birds

VIC: He's a bird watcher.

TERRY: Eh? You a peeping tom, are you?

VIC: Now that explains a lot. All those nude orgies in the basement, yes, all fits, don't it?

PAUL: None of your business. You're hooligans.

(To VIC*)*

You should have more sense, you're old enough. What do you think you're doing leading him on like this? Think it's funny, do you? Well, I'll tell you, if you try to stop me leaving once more, once more, I shall fetch the police. You're breaking the law. *(Pause.)* Right.

*(*PAUL *attempts to push through to the door but* VIC *grabs his arm and thrusts it up his back.* PAUL *yells with pain.)*

VIC: Quiet! Quiet. That's it, squire. *(To* TERRY:*)* Rope. *(To* PAUL:*)* Now, all we're going to do is sit down again. *(He forces* PAUL *into the chair.)* There. Yes. Comfy? Good.

*(*TERRY *brings a length of rope and gives it to* VIC. TERRY *stands over* PAUL *with his chain poised to strike.)*

VIC: My advice is – keep still. *(He ties* PAUL *to the chair.)*

PAUL: What are you doing?

VIC: Well, squire, you're up and down like a whore's drawers. Wear yourself out. So, we'll just make you comfy, then we can talk.

PAUL: Look, I don't want to cause trouble, so don't force me to get the police. Let's forget it.

VIC: I have already.

PAUL: Just let me go and we'll say no more about it.

VIC: You see, Inspector, we happen to be highly disturbed by the numbers of people who condemn others simply because of their appearance. For instance, in face of our hospitality you have used words like yobbo and hooligan, and I would stress that Mister Breedon has been most upset. Simply because his hair is short while yours is long, because he prefers braces to a belt and happens to enjoy wearing boots – are these reasons to condemn him? I would hardly think so, not in your tolerant society. I

2	a peeping tom *(sl.)* ['pi:pɪŋ 'tɒm]	a man who secretly watches women undressing
12	to thrust [θrʌst]	to push hard
	to yell	to utter a loud, sharp cry
17	poised to strike [pɔɪzd]	held ready to strike
20	a whore [hɔ:]	a prostitute
	(a pair of) drawers	old word for (under)pants *(Unterhose, Schlüpfer)*
	to wear oneself out	to exhaust oneself, to get tired

mean to say, Grenadier Guardsmen crop their heads, wear braces, boots, *and* fight, for *money*! Paid for it. And yet find society's approval. But Mister Breedon here, my blood brother, it's most confusing, can't get him into a detention centre quick enough. That rope not too tight, is it?

PAUL: Please ...

VIC *(to* TERRY *quietly)*: Scissors.

PAUL: What?

VIC: Just a word to my friend. *(*TERRY *crosses to the wardrobe to collect scissors.)* I mean, what makes Mister Breedon, or me, a yobbo and not you? What could that be?

PAUL: All right, I'm sorry for saying –

VIC: Too late, squire! Keep still.

PAUL: I want to go.

VIC *(taking the scissors from* TERRY*)*: You see, from where we're sitting, you and your mates are a highly privileged mob. All laid on up there in your university, innit? Study, recreation, all your arts, films, holidays abroad, swimming-pool, bars, dances, crumpet galore, restaurant ... all paid! All this and well paid just to get your head in a book or two, so you'll be well equipped to pick up your fifty a week, for starters. And very very nice too. Yes. Congratulations. *(He snips at* PAUL*'s hair.)*

PAUL: Here, what's going on?

VIC: Just a trim, squire.

PAUL *(struggling, shouts)*: Help! Help! Somebody get the police. Help! *(*VIC *grabs* PAUL*'s hair and forces his head back. He points the scissors at* his throat. PAUL *stares, terrified.)*

VIC: Quiet. You hear me? One more peep out of you and Mister Breedon lays into you – chain, boot, the lot. Savvy? Got that?

1	a Grenadier Guardsman ['grenədɪə 'gɑ:dzmən]	a soldier in the Grenadier Guards, a British regiment
4	a detention centre [dɪ'tenʃn]	a place where young offenders or criminals are kept (usually for a short time)
15	a mob	a crowd
	all laid on	everything (is) provided
17	galore [gə'lɔ:]	in plenty; in large amounts or numbers
19	for starters *(sl.)*	to begin with
22	a trim	a (hair) cut
26	a peep *(coll.)*	a sound
27	to lay into s.o. *(coll.)*	to attack s.o. violently
	the lot *(coll.)*	everything
	Savvy? ['sævɪ] *(sl.)*	Understand?

PAUL *(whimpers)*: Please.

VIC *(cutting* PAUL's *hair)*: Just a trim, professor.

PAUL: Done nothing to you ... to anybody. I'm non-violent.

VIC: And I doubt if you ever give a thought to the likes of Mister Breedon, do you? Of course not. Why should you? Course, if you'd seen the rathole he was dragged up in, seen the area, school run by cane-happy pigs, Catholics as a matter of fact, and parents not quite genteel – you may have been momentarily shocked. No, Mr Breedon did not have a lot to look forward to. The jobs open to him, you might imagine – no chance for him, no plush university seat – ending up with his picture on the mantelpiece – cap and gown and his proud mum and dad, smiling, clutching his chit, set nicely, on the ladder, eh? No. Not for him. And he's not so different from you. Not that much. He's young, got energy, gets bored easy – except he hasn't got a bloody chance. So he gets rid of his juices, through bovver. Should he know better? Eh? Is there something else he should do? Are there provisions? No. No, Mr Breedon does not like students. And Mister Breedon particularly dislikes students who call him 'hooligan' and 'yobbo'.

*(*PAUL *sits with his head slumped forward.* VIC *has cropped off most of his hair.)*

VIC: There. What do you think, Terry?

TERRY: Shave. Shave it.

VIC: Oh, no, I think no.

*(*TERRY *indicates his boots and points at* PAUL. VIC *nods.* TERRY *takes off his boots, pulls off* PAUL's *shoes and puts the boots on* PAUL's *feet.)*

VIC *(admiringly)*: Oh yes. Yes. Nice. Chic. Untie him *(*TERRY *unties the rope.* PAUL *sits motionless.)* All right, squire.

1	to whimper ['wɪmpə]	to utter weak, plaintive sounds
6	cane-happy	happy to use canes *(Rohrstock)* to punish pupils
7	genteel [dʒen'ti:l]	belonging to a high social class
10	plush [plʌʃ]	comfortable, luxurious
11	**mantelpiece** ['mæntlpi:s]	a shelf above the fireplace *(Kaminsims)*
	cap and gown [gaʊn]	traditional clothes worn by British students on graduation day (i.e. after their final examinations)
	to clutch s.th. [klʌtʃ]	to hold s.th. tightly
12	a chit [tʃɪt]	*here:* degree (document)
14	juices	*here:* superfluous energy
15	bovver *(sl.)*	*here:* fighting, aggressive behaviour
16	provisions	*here:* possibilities, arrangements
19	to slump [slʌmp]	to fall down heavily

*(*TERRY *pokes* PAUL.*)*

PAUL *(quietly)*: I'm reporting this to the police.

VIC: Sorry, Doctor – we'll be there first. Complain about the noise. Your orgies. Have you evicted. Not half. And you haven't been here this afternoon. We haven't seen you. Two against one. Sorry.

*(*TERRY *pokes* PAUL. PAUL *stands up.)*

VIC: Oh, très chic. Have a butchers in the mirror, squire, you look a treat.

*(*TERRY *pushes* PAUL *towards the mirror.* PAUL *stands and looks at himself. His face contorts with rage.* VIC *laughs,* TERRY *sniggers.)*

TERRY: Ponce.

*(*PAUL *breaks. He grabs a broom and thrashes about the room. He lays* VIC *out with a single blow. He smashes up the room. The bicycle chain flies out of* TERRY'S *hand during the mêlée and he cowers away from the frenetic* PAUL. PAUL *calms down, but he is trembling and on the verge of tears. He picks up the bicycle chain and crosses to stand over* TERRY. TERRY *raises his arm to defend himself.)*

PAUL: Nothing ... did nothing ... non-violent. You ... you ...

(He drops his arm and crosses to the chair. He takes off the boots and puts on his own shoes. He slowly exits. TERRY *crosses to kneel beside* VIC.*)*

TERRY: Vic ... Vic ... here ... Vic ...

1	to poke s.o. [pəʊk]	to push s.o. with a finger or a pointed object
4	to evict s.o. [ɪ'vɪkt]	to force s.o. to move out of a house by law
	not half *(coll.)*	indeed
7	You look a treat. [tri:t]	You look great, fantastic.
9	to contort [kən'tɔ:t]	to twist, to get deformed
10	a ponce *(sl.)*	a man who controls prostitutes
11	to thrash about [θræʃ]	to move around wildly and violently
	to lay s.o. out	to knock s.o. unconscious
12	to smash s.th. up	to break s.th. to pieces
13	a mêlée ['meleɪ]	a confused fight or struggle
	to cower ['kaʊə]	to bend down or move back because of fear

Biographical Notes

Roy Minton was born in Nottingham in 1933. He was the eldest of 13 children. Soon his career turned out to be rather unusual. At the age of 15 he left home. Later he spent three years "working against, rather than for, the Royal Air Force" (as he put it) in the Middle East and Malaya. He then worked in a number of jobs such as coalminer, waiter in a restaurant, labourer, cornflake packer, stoker in a tug boat, and clerk in an office. After some experience in a repertory company in which he acted in a variety of plays, he studied drama at the Guildhall School of Music and Drama. Afterwards he returned to acting not only in theatre, but also on radio and television.

Roy Minton wrote a number of plays and was awarded the first BBC bursary (= scholarship) for playwriting in 1966. His works include *Gentleman Caller, You've Got a Lucky Face, The Hunting of Lionel Crane, Ben, Horace, Nobby's Turn, Good Times, The Gold Medallist, Death in Leicester* and *Scum*.

Bovver was especially written for the "Everyman Theatre" in Liverpool and was published in a collection of plays in 1976. It deals with the problem of social dissatisfaction among young people resulting in aggression and violence.

Unterrichtsvorschläge

Vorbemerkungen

1. Inhalt

In einer schlecht eingerichteten und mit provokativer Dekoration versehenen Ein-Zimmer-Wohnung hausen Vic und Terry. Vic, Anfang 30, untersetzt, stämmig, breitschultrig und mit großen Händen versehen, scheint dem Arbeitermilieu zu entstammen. Die Art jedoch, wie er sich sprachlich und argumentativ bewegen kann, legt die Vermutung nahe, daß er ein intellektueller Drop-out ist. Seine feindselige Ablehnung der etablierten Gesellschaft gegenüber kann er geradezu virtuos offen und verdeckt handhaben. Er ist äußerst redegewandt und verfügt über eine Schlagfertigkeit, die man oft bei intelligenten Leuten aus sozial benachteiligten Milieus findet. Während seine Aggressivität psychologisch-raffiniert und intellektuell-verbal ist, äußert sie sich bei Terry, einem 18jährigen Skinhead, dumpf und physisch-brutal. Das ungleiche Paar vereint nicht nur ihre Arbeitslosigkeit, sondern auch das Bedürfnis nach Provokation, um ihre Frustration abzureagieren (cf. 'So he gets rid of his juices, through bovver'; **63** 14–15). Gleich zu Beginn versuchen sie deshalb, ihre Mitbewohner durch unglaublichen Lärm herauszufordern. Sie haben Erfolg. Ihr Opfer ist der Student Paul, 'a second-year student, an ordinary, gentle young man, slim, with longish hair but not overdone. He wears spectacles' (**46** 20–22). Paul ist das ideale Angriffsziel ihres aufgestauten Hasses: Er stammt aus bürgerlichem Milieu, hat eine vielversprechende Zukunft und *non-violence* als politische Zielvorstellung.

Pauls pazifistische Prinzipien werden gleich von Anfang an einer schweren Prüfung unterzogen. Er will sich – und damit fängt die dramatische Handlung an – eigentlich über den Lärm beschweren, wird jedoch daran gehindert, sein Anliegen vorzubringen. Vic unterbricht ihn und lenkt ihn ständig ab, wobei er seine Aggressivität in einem ironisch-höflichen Rollenspiel so raffiniert versteckt, daß Paul wie hypnotisiert erscheint. Als dieser seiner Beschwerde endlich Gehör verschafft, wird der Spieß umgedreht. Vic argwöhnt, daß Paul wohl von der Polizei sei, Radiolizenzen zu kontrollieren habe oder vielleicht gar – als guter Bürger – Einbrechern auf der Spur sei. Paul fühlt sich allmählich unwohl in seiner Haut. Er will sich zurückziehen, wird jedoch von Terrys physischer Präsenz daran gehindert. Er wird gezwungen, sich auf einen unbequemen Stuhl ('the upright chair'; **51** 5) zu setzen und wird immer mehr wie ein Angeklagter behandelt. Vic spielt zunächst die Rolle eines Psychiaters, der Paul zu unterstellen versucht, daß er geisteskrank sei. Danach macht er sich nicht nur zum bürgerlich-moralischen Richter über Pauls angebliche Ruhestörungen und homosexuelle Orgien, sondern agiert zugleich als Ankläger, als Opfer und als Zeuge. Der Druck auf Paul wird immer größer, verstärkt durch Terrys Drohgebärden mit einer Fahrradkette. Paul versucht noch einmal zu entfliehen, wird aber daraufhin an seinen Stuhl gefesselt. Er wehrt sich verzweifelt, kann aber seiner Bestrafung nicht entkommen. Vic läßt seine Maske fallen und verbalisiert seinen Haß auf die privilegierten Studenten ('a highly privileged mob'; **62** 15). Gerade sie haben kein Recht, auf ihn und Terry arrogant herabzuschauen. Er nimmt an Paul Rache für die Ungerechtigkeit der Gesellschaft: Paul wird zum Skinhead gemacht, indem Vic ihm die Haare abschneidet und Terry ihm seine Stiefel anzieht. Als er schließlich losgebunden wird, hat er sein „Spiegelerlebnis" ('towards the mirror ... looks at himself'; **64** 8). Er kennt sich nicht mehr und gerät außer sich. In frenetischer Wut streckt er Vic nieder, zerstört das ganze Zimmer und hält erst dann völlig bestürzt inne, als er Terry mit der Fahrradkette attackieren will. Er ist fassungslos ob seiner eigenen Aggressivität, die, wie seine gestammelten Worte '... did nothing – non-violent ...' (**64** 17) andeuten, eine völlig neue Erfahrung für ihn darstellt. Auch er ist zum *bovver* fähig und im Grunde ein *blood brother* von Vic und Terry. Während Terry sich um den verletzten Vic kümmert, zieht Paul seine Schuhe wieder an und verläßt gebrochen den Ort des Geschehens.

2. Thematische Aspekte

Bovver exemplifiziert die gattungsspezifischen Merkmale eines *short play* in besonders deutlicher Weise. Das Drama bietet daher eine Fülle von Sprechanlässen über die auf die Krisen- und Endsituation ausgerichtete Handlung, über das optisch auf das Wesentliche konzentrierte Bühnenbild, über die sprachliche Einheit und Atmosphäre und nicht zuletzt über den offenen Schluß. Gesprächsanlässe bietet auch die plastische Darstellung der beiden Hauptcharaktere Vic und Paul – sie sind fast schon *round characters* –, sowie deren Rollentausch am Ende. Das Drama ist darüber hinaus voller Spannung, deren schrittweiser Aufbau von den Schülern verbalisiert werden kann und die sich im vorliegenden Unterrichtsmodell in den Tafelbildern widerspiegelt.

Inhaltlich schneidet *Bovver* eine Reihe von Themenbereichen an:

1. Das Werk ist eine literarische Darstellung des Themas „Aggression" als Grundphänomen menschlicher Existenz. Der Begriff dürfte den Schülern aus anderen Fachbereichen (z. B. Biologie), bzw. aus eigener Erfahrung bekannt sein. Im Vergleich zwischen Realität und literarischer Sublimierung können sie sich auseinandersetzen mit Vics subtiler Verbal-Aggression einerseits, sowie mit Terrys direkter Brachialgewalt andererseits. Darüber hinaus ergibt sich die Frage nach der Manipulierbarkeit des Menschen: Können Menschen in eine solch ausweglose Situation getrieben werden, daß sie jede Form von anerzogener Verhaltensweise abstreifen und

sich letztlich nur noch animalisch-instinktiv verhalten? *Bovver* würde sich also gut als literarischer Text im Rahmen einer Unterrichtseinheit über *aggression, violence (brainwashing), crime* (u. U. *city problems*) anbieten.

2. Die Lebensweise und „Philosophie" der Skinheads, deren Beziehung zur Arbeiterklasse, ihre Uniformität, ihre *obsession with territory* im Hinblick auf die *coloured immigrants*, überhaupt ihr Feindbild-Denken (*'us' vs 'them'*) werden im Drama teilweise bis ins Detail verdeutlicht und thematisiert. Das Werk kann also gut im Zusammenhang mit Themenbereichen wie *youth styles, subcultures, social classes, protest of society* eingesetzt werden.

3. Vic bewegt sich souverän auf allen Sprachebenen. Die Mixtur zwischen *standard* und *sub-standard English*, von *slang* und *colloquial English* bis hin zum Gebrauch von *taboo*-Wörtern, bietet die Möglichkeit, den Themenbereich „soziale Schicht und Sprache" zu behandeln. Das könnte auch das Phänomen einschließen, daß sich das Sprachverhalten aufgrund von physischem und psychischem Druck erheblich verändern kann. So verläßt z. B. Paul unter Druck immer mehr sein *standard English.*

4. Ein weiteres Thema ist die Relativität der Rechtssprechung im Drama. Vic und Terry haben die Macht und beanspruchen deshalb auch das moralische Recht auf *law and order*, obgleich sie – wie der Zuschauer weiß – schlichtweg lügen ('Radio, in this room? There's been some mistake, surely.'; **49** 13–14) und die gesamte Gerichtsprozedur pervertieren. In diesem Sinn eignet sich *Bovver* auch als satirisch-literarische Ergänzung zu Themenbereichen wie *law, legal procedure, justice, torture, punishment* (u. U. *Amnesty International*).

3. Methodische Hinweise

Die vorliegenden Unterrichtsvorschläge teilen das Drama in einzelne *teaching units* ein, die so bemessen sind, daß jeweils ein bis zwei *units* pro Stunde behandelt werden können. Sie zielen darauf ab, die Lektüre möglichst abwechslungsreich und flexibel zu gestalten. Die vorgeschlagenen Leitfragen können gemeinsam durch fragend-entwickelndes Verfahren beantwortet oder als Arbeitsaufträge (Gruppenarbeit) vergeben werden. Zur Ergebnissicherung werden Tafelbilder vorgeschlagen, die natürlich je nach Unterrichtsverlauf variiert werden können und sollten und die auch auf Folie oder Arbeitsblätter übertragbar sind.

Die Anordnung der einzelnen Unterrichtsabschnitte spiegelt den dramatischen Verlauf von *Bovver* wider. Dieses Vorgehen bietet sich nicht nur aufgrund des Umfangs des Dramas an, sondern auch wegen des relativ starken Gebrauchs von *slang*. Es ist deshalb empfehlenswert, das Textverständnis durch das Lesen des Texts (einzeln/gemeinsam/in Rollen) unter Zuhilfenahme der Worterklärungen abzusichern und erst dann die Cassette einzusetzen.

Die Cassettenaufnahme kann natürlich zur Schulung des Hörverständnisses auch gleich eingesetzt werden. Gerade Vics Stimme ist außerordentlich realitätsnah, weil sie über den Gebrauch des *slang* und des *formal English* hinaus den emotionalen Abläufen der Dialoge besonders deutlich durch eine variable Stimmführung Ausdruck verleiht.

Der Einstieg in die Behandlung des Dramas kann direkt über die Analyse der Bühnenanweisungen sowie der *dumb show* (**45** 14–**46** 15) erfolgen (vgl. Unit 1). Andererseits können die im Drama abgesteckten Themenbereiche, wie z. B. Skinheads und Aggression durch verschiedene – möglichst personalisierte – Texte vorbereitet werden, um die Schüler für die relevanten Probleme und Fragestellungen zu sensibilisieren.

4. *Bovver* als Theaterstück

Das vorliegende Drama ist schon mehrfach und sehr erfolgreich durch englische Theater-AGs an deutschen Schulen aufgeführt worden. Die Zahl der Schauspieler ist begrenzt. Es bedarf relativ weniger *stage props*. Der Einstieg (*dumb show*) ist für alle Zuschauer verständlich. Ebenso können auch Zuschauer mit weniger Englischkenntnissen der eindeutig auf den Höhepunkt abzielenden Handlung folgen, wenn – wie geschehen – der Handlungsablauf und eine Reihe von *slang*-Ausdrücken auf Deutsch auf einem besonderen Blatt erklärt werden, das vor der Aufführung ausgeteilt wird.

Unit 1: The Stage Directions (**45** 1–**46** 22)

Am Anfang steht die genaue Lektüre der Bühnenanweisungen mit dem Ziel, das Bühnenbild und dessen spezielle Aufgabe für das Kurzdrama darzustellen (u. U. kann das Bühnenbild gezeichnet werden). Auf jeden Fall sollte das Werk zunächst nicht als Wortkunstwerk, sondern als Bühnenkunstwerk erfaßt werden, da der Zuschauer die von der Bühne ausgehenden Signale automatisch interpretiert und sie in die Gesamtaussage einbezieht. Das gilt auch für die Pantomime, die das dramatische Geschehen eröffnet.

1. *What information is conveyed by the state of Vic and Terry's room, and what is its dramatic function?*

The extensive stage directions provide the reader (audience) with the atmosphere and the mood of the play. They give a detailed description of the room where Vic and Terry live. Not only is the room used for both living and sleeping in; it also contains only a few pieces of furniture, all of which are in poor condition. Everything seems to be shabby, worn out, tawdry and untidy. Terry and Vic live in poverty and in a miserable and pitiable state. But – not surprisingly – they just don't care.

Suggestions for the blackboard:

Vic and Terry's room	implications
– ground-floor bedsitter – a few pieces of furniture – shabbily furnished room – battered easy chairs – cheap, worn suitcases – room not dressed – tatty carpets – pile of bedding & carpets in room	– Terry and Vic live in poverty – in a miserable and pitiable state – wretched conditions – they don't care about their surroundings or feel responsible for the state of their room
	Everything reflects their psychological state

2. *What elements of provocation is the audience confronted with at the beginning of the play (**45** 7–20)?*
At the beginning of the play there is a dumb show. Vic and Terry don't speak, they only mime their actions. But their behaviour and gestures signify contempt and aggressiveness. One almost feels that they'll soon turn to active aggression. The provocative tension is intensified by further elements, such as the way the room is furnished or the outward appearance of Terry. Both Terry and Vic are obviously in conflict with society.

Suggestions for the blackboard:

general symbols of provocation	Vic and Terry's behaviour
– nude pin-ups – German helmet and flag – large picture of Hitler – cropped hair, braces and boots } skinhead fashion	– eat chips from paper – throw paper in the wardrobe – suck teeth, smack lips
they are in conflict with society (obscenity, radicalism, provocative clothes and hair-style)	bad manners = provocation

The theme of skinheads should preferably not be discussed until more information about Terry is given (cf. Unit 8).

3. *How do Vic and Terry provoke Paul, the student downstairs, and why do they tidy up their room?*
For no apparent reason, the quiet, almost relaxed atmosphere suddenly changes dramatically. Vic and Terry act provocatively by making a deafening noise which doesn't abate until they hear someone coming upstairs. At

once they act in great haste and tidy up their room. Vic assumes control by checking the room and hushing Terry. Before Paul enters, a hurried attempt is made to give the appearance of order and decency and thereby to assume respectability.

Suggestions for the blackboard:

provocation of Paul	➡ false pretences: respectability
Vic and Terry ... – bang broom handles on the floor – crash their boots – stamp up and down – turn on radio loudly	They ... – dash to hide brooms – switch off and hide radio – carry bedding to bed and spread it tidily – spread carpet on floor – reverse picture of Hitler (Queen Elizabeth on the other side)
DEAFENING NOISE	⇨ SILENCE, HASTE, SECRECY

4. *Give examples of the various theatrical devices that arouse the audience's interest at the beginning of the play.*
Curiosity is aroused by a series of contradictory actions and situations.
- calm atmosphere – deafening noise – silence and haste (suspense)
- room in a mess (in accordance with Terry and Vic's way of life), then suddenly tidied up (surprise)
- broom not used to clean the room with, but to make a noise (surprise)
- radio used as an instrument of provocation (taken out from under the floorboard) (surprise)
- picture of Hitler reversed: Queen Elizabeth on the reverse (surprise).

Homework:
Summarize the main elements of the stage directions (introduction of place, characters; creation of suspense).

Unit 2: Paul's Reception (**46** 23–**48** 23)

In diesem Teil geht es um die Begrüßung von Paul durch Vic und Terry, die anfangs sehr höflich erscheint, sich dann aber als spannungsgeladen und bedrohlich herausstellt.

Es empfiehlt sich, zunächst den Text zu lesen, daran anschließend (mehrfach) die Cassette zu hören, bevor an Hand der folgenden Fragen die Leitlinien des Eröffnunsdialogs verfolgt werden.

1. *How does Vic greet Paul and what role does he play?*
According to his outward appearance and the fact that he lives together with Terry one would expect Vic to use 'bad' or substandard English and to behave rudely. But surprisingly he pretends to be very polite and invites Paul to come in ('Be my guest'). He also uses the formal and carefully phrased (even at times literary) English of the upper-middle class and pretends to live in wealth and prosperity – with all its 'ever so terrible' problems (e. g. 'with the staff'; **47** 9). It is like an ironic cat-and-mouse game with Paul as the victim.

The students can easily make a list of the passages that show Vic's assumed role.

Suggestions for the blackboard:

'Come in … Be my guest.' 'You'd insult us?' '… come in. Do.'	*hearty welcome*	Vic's role play ↓
– 'I don't think we've been introduced' – He ignores handshake, bows only. – 'Mister Owen … Mister Terry Breedon.'	*formal manners*	
– 'I'm a stickler for procedure' – 'definite proclivity for the formalities of life' – 'as you might comprehend' – 'Rather partial to formality' – 'don't want any aspersions cast on the quality of our hospitality'	*formal language*	
– 'Butler's day off. Terrible problems with staff'	*pretended upper-class wealth*	

Vic doesn't entirely stick to his assumed role. He sometimes uses colloquialisms, slang and substandard English ('COMFY, ARE YOU?'; **48** 15; 'bloody awful'; **47** 10; 'Don't go for the flashing bit'; **48** 11; 'bum'; **48** 17), the result of which is a strange mixture of levels on which he approaches Paul.

2. *Give examples of Vic and Terry's aggressiveness*
After the first polite, preliminary words of welcome Paul is given orders ('Sit down'; **46** 29, **47** 1/5) and later on even shouted at ('COMFY, ARE YOU?'; **48** 15). He is also interrupted so that he is unable to make any complaints about the noise. Furthermore Vic puts on a threatening smile

and ignores Paul's handshake. Terry stares coldly at him. At the beginning Paul is pulled inside (Vic closes the door) and soon forced to sit in an upright chair in the centre of the room. In this position he will indeed be the target for Vic's show of aggression and the chair will turn out to be the place of the accused. There is a hidden force and aggression in Vic's and Terry's words, gestures and actions, intensified by Vic's feigned politeness. He addresses Paul mockingly as 'monsieur' (**46** 23), 'effendi' (**46** 27), 'squire' (**47** 1), 'sahib' (**47** 5) and 'señor' (**47** 21). Eventually Paul is compelled to play a ridiculous role: he has to introduce himself officially and tell Vic he lives downstairs, which is commented on coldly ('I'm well aware of that, señor. Yes, indeed'; **47** 21).

Suggestions for the blackboard:

Vic's aggression	↗ **PAUL** ↖	**Terry's aggression**
– calls him sahib, señor, squire, effendi, monsieur – gives orders – shouts at Paul – interrupts Paul	words	– threatening silence
– threatening smile – ignores handshake	gestures	– stares at Paul coldly
– pulls Paul inside – closes door – forces Paul on upright chair	actions	– sits in easy chair

3. *Describe Paul's reaction*
Paul feels embarrassed and awkward. At first he is polite. He apologizes for his intrusion; but soon he finds out that it is difficult to get into normal contact with Vic (and Terry). He is often interrupted and his attempts at making Vic listen to him fail ('Look, Vic ...'; **47** 11). He offers his hand, which is coldly ignored. There is no way he can escape from the situation he unexpectedly finds himself in. He is forced to obey Vic's orders and to stay longer than intended. And finally, feeling more and more uneasy, he adjusts to the situation as best he can and even pretends to feel comfortable.

The students could be handed a worksheet (see overleaf) with the information in the left-hand column given; their task would be to outline Paul's gradual adjustment to the situation as suggested in the right-hand column:

Paul's reaction	
'Sorry to disturb you but –' (**46** 24)	apologizes
'Just wanted to say, ask –' (**46** 26) 'I just thought, I'd heard –' (**47** 16) 'Well, it was the noise –' (**48** 12)	tries to complain politely
'Look, Vic' (**47** 11) 'I'm, er, I'm Paul.' (**47** 20) Offers hand. (**47** 23)	tries to get in contact
'No. I won't stay.' (**46** 30) 'Yes, well, for a moment.' (**47** 2) 'Shouldn't really.' (**47** 6) Sits. (**47** 7)	obeys
'Yes, yes thanks.' (**48** 16) 'This is fine.' (**48** 19)	pretends to feel comfortable
	embarrassed

Homework:
What is the relation between Vic and Terry?
They live together and have the same skinhead 'ideals'. They are even 'blood brothers' and have similar tatoos (eagles in flight!). Vic is much older than Terry and the dominant one of the two. He is intelligent and 'monopolizes' the conversation. Terry is sullen and dangerous and supports Vic's verbal aggression with threatening gestures. They are interdependent, each acting as a foil to the other: Terry is Vic's 'protégé', and Terry acts like Vic's bodyguard.

Unit 3: Paul's Complaint (**49** 1–**51** 5)

In diesem Teil gelingt es Paul schließlich, seine Beschwerde wegen Lärmbelästigung vorzubringen. Vic argwöhnt und unterstellt, daß Paul wohl von der Polizei sei und Radiolizenzen zu überprüfen habe. Paul wird die Situation langsam unangenehm. Er will gehen, woran er gewaltsam gehindert wird.

Unterrichtsvorschlag:

Erarbeiten dieses Teils in Stillarbeit, anschließend Anhören der Aufnahme. Diese lebt von der Spannung zwischen Vics leichtem Cockney-Akzent und der von seiner Wortwahl eigentlich zu erwartenden *received pronunciation.*

1. *What does Paul want and how does he put forward his request? What is his situation at the end of this phase?*
Although intimidated, Paul repeats his polite request to stop the noise ('Don't like to complain'; **49** 5; 'if you could, just a little quieter'; **49** 8–9) by appealing to fairness ('we give and take'; **49** 8) and by giving reasons ('a lot of work'; **49** 9; 'concentration'; **49** 11). But this doesn't help. Vic defends himself rather aggressively and Paul soon realizes that it is no use arguing logically ('Look, have your joke ...,'; **49** 21). He wants to terminate the argument and leave. He gradually gives up his politeness and expresses his anger. Considering the direct threat posed by Terry, Paul shows considerable courage: 'I haven't time to listen to you rambling on' (**50** 10); 'Who do you think you're –' (**50** 20); 'I'll watch what I think fit' (**50** 25). But when Vic and Terry become more and more aggressive, he is hopelessly at a loss. In fact, at the end of this part Paul is treated like a dog ('Heel!'; **51** 1). He is trapped and frightened.

2. *Describe Vic's reaction towards Paul's complaint.*
At first Vic pretends not to understand Paul (**49** 4). Then he denies having a radio (thus telling a downright lie) before starting a sort of 'counter-attack'. He accuses Paul of having some connection with the police (**49** 22–**50** 9). Everything is aimed at subtly attacking Paul's identity and limiting his personal liberty. Vic calls him 'inspector' (**50** 9), pretends to have forgotten his name (**50** 21), shouts at him, is even ready to fight (*'rolls up his shirt sleeves'*, **50** 13) and forces him to sit on the upright chair by treating him like a dog ('Heel!'; **51** 1/3; *'prods him in the chest'*; **51** 4). There is also a strange game of 'hide and seek': Vic 'hides' behind Terry ('Terry didn't like that'; **50** 14), warns him of Terry, who indeed intervenes at that signal (**50** 19/26). Judging from the various names he addresses Paul with, one might conclude that Vic is not interested in Paul as an individual: Paul seems to be the personified object of his general disgust at 'students'.

The answers to questions 1 and 2 can be summed up on the board like this (see overleaf):

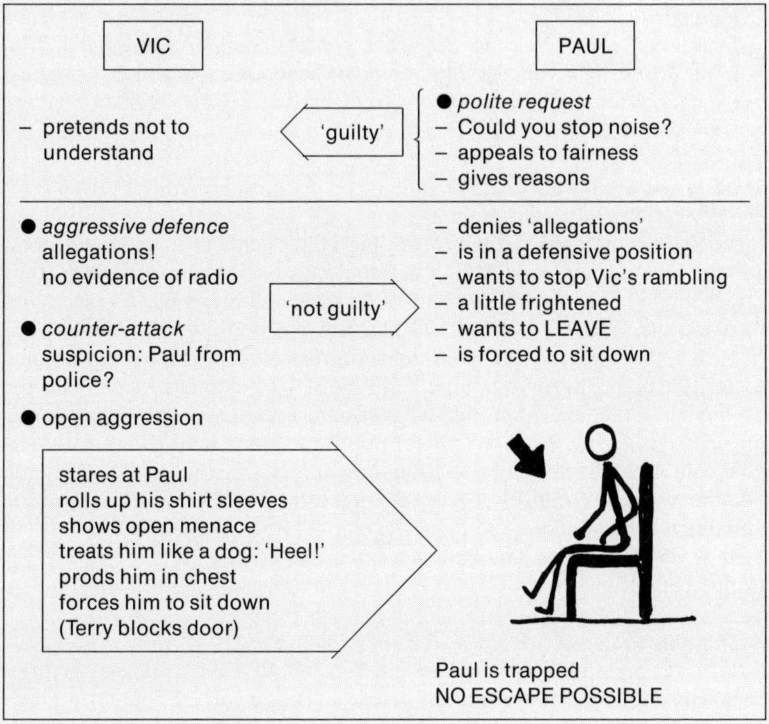

Unit 4: Vic's Defence – Paul is Cornered (**51** 6–**52** 26)

Dieser Teil ist die direkte Fortsetzung des vorhergehenden Abschnitts. Paul sieht sich weiteren Angriffen ausgesetzt und kann nicht mehr entfliehen.

Unterrichtsvorschlag: Auch diesen Teil erarbeiten die Schüler selbst, indem sie den Text nicht nur lesen, sondern auch versuchen, Vics aggressive Verteidigung und Pauls Reaktionen darauf in Form einer Gegenüberstellung aufzulisten (analog zum vorhergehenden Tafelbild). Danach kann die Cassette gehört werden.

1. *Describe Vic's vicious defence and Paul's reaction to it.*
Vic 'ties' Paul to the upright (!) chair by increasingly assuming the role of a judge who treats it as a 'case' (**51** 16) and accuses Paul of false accusations (**51** 12–13, **52** 1–2/24). Paul, on the other hand, tries to defend himself ('I'm

not accusing anybody'; **51** 15; 'Not accusation!'; **52** 25) and to tell Vic that he doesn't believe him. ('You know damn well what was going on!'; **52** 9). Vic then starts a subtle form of torture. Not only does he again play the role of a member of the upper class, whose language is used as a satire on upper-class mannerisms, but he also attacks Paul psychologically. He calls him 'Mister Whatsit' (**51** 9, **52** 11), pretends to be taken aback by his bad language (**52** 10), mocks his education by surreptitiously jeering at his 'being an intellectual' and having a 'superior knowledge' and an 'immeasurable vocabulary' (**52** 17–19). He even starts a mock defence in favour of the accused (**52** 10). Paul is desperate (**51** 20, **52** 3) and wants to withdraw, but is unable to leave. He is 'tied' to the chair tighter than ever before, because suddenly Terry stands behind (!) him (**52** 16). He is wedged in tightly between the two.

Suggestions for the blackboard:

VIC

- **adopts various roles**
  (= 'law and order')
  - judge
    - treats it as a case
    - accuses Paul of allegations
  - pretends to be upper class
    (formal language)
- **attacks Paul psychologically**
  - calls him 'Mister Whatsit'
  - reproaches him for using bad language
  - mocks his education
  - mock defence of Paul (**52** 10–15)
    (He might have come up because of burglars.)

Vic veils his own identity (roles) and mocks Paul's identity.

PAUL

(Terry behind Paul)

- wants to drop his complaint
- tries to defend himself
- stares at the floor, resigned, confused
- moans, sighs
- wants to LEAVE

Paul cannot escape.

2. *What is the function of the pause at the end?*

The pause at the end of this scene is important from the dramatic point of view. Vic pauses for breath before making a new and even more severe attack, whereas Paul and the audience must recover their breath.

Homework:

Read ***52*** *27–57 15 and try and describe Vic's psychological warfare in this part of the play.* (Suggested answer: see Unit 5, pp 146–147.)

Unit 5: Vic's Counter-attack (**52** 57–**55** 15)

In diesem Teil wird Paul durch einen psychologischen Gegenangriff immer mehr in die Enge getrieben.

Es empfiehlt sich, vor dem Anhören der Cassette (wo zusätzliche Geräusche und Terrys Gelächter zu hören sind) den Text zunächst zu lesen (vgl. Vorschlag *Homework, Unit 4,* S. 145).

1. *Describe Vic's aggressive assaults on Paul.*

Vic applies psychological warfare by using the carrot and stick method. On the one hand he forces Paul to apologize, on the other hand he pretends to help him by guiding him with gestures and confidential whispers (**53** 21–24). He also uses Terry to threaten Paul (**53** 12–14), and yet protects Paul from a possible attack by Terry ('Gently, blood brother.'; **53** 18). In addition to this he makes fun of him by using a lot of names ('Mister Whatsit'; **53** 29; 'Doctor (Watson)'; **54** 1–3) and suspects him of being a psychiatric case (**52** 28, **53** 3–4/28, **55** 2).

2. *How does Terry behave?*

Terry has so far hardly said a word. He now stands behind Paul's chair and represents to a certain extent Vic's 'executive force'. In a tyrannical outburst Terry suddenly shouts at Paul to make him answer Vic's question whether he is having psychiatric treatment (**53** 1). Eventually he forces Paul to apologize by threatening him with physical violence (**53** 15–17). He treats him with skinhead contempt for students (**55** 9).

3. *Describe Paul's situation*

Paul is hopelessly exposed to Vic's verbal aggressions and derision and Terry's physical threats. At first he is impatient and annoyed. ('PAUL *sighs, exasperated.*'; **52** 29). But these first signs of aggression are suppressed immediately by Terry's despotic demands ('Answer!'; **53** 1/8; 'Apologize!'; **53** 15/20) and the fact that he is standing behind him. Vic's psychological treatment eventually leads Paul to gesture helplessly with his hands before getting his words out (**55** 3). He begins to sound almost insane – which he is not. Paul can now only take refuge from Vic by referring to his role as a student ('I'm a student, second-year ...'; **55** 3). He can only 'survive' by reassuring himself; otherwise he would be lost.

The answers to questions 1–3 could be summed up on the board like this:

Vic

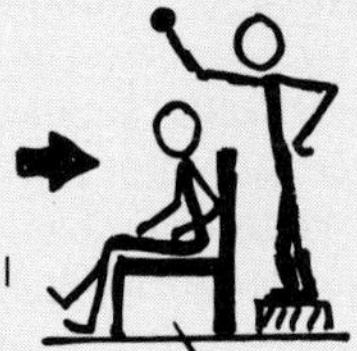

- *'carrot and stick' approach*
  - forces and 'helps' Paul to apologize
  - warns Paul of Terry and protects him
- *names*
  Paul = Mister Whatsit
  Doctor Watson
  (Sherlock's fiancé)
- *Paul – a psychiatric case?*
  hallucinations?
  mental disorder?
  schizophrenic?

Vic's psychological attack

Terry (the watchdog)

- poses a physical threat
- puts in his share of torture: 'Apologize!'
- treats Paul with contempt: 'Student!'

Paul

- sighs, is exasperated
- is forced to apologize
- looks for guidance
- wants to go
- gestures helplessly with hand

Paul's only help is his role ('I'm a student, second year ...'; **55** 3)

Homework

*How does Vic criticize and ridicule psychiatric treatment? (Refer to **54** 1–**55** 1).*

Vic's general comment on psychiatric treatment is quite an intelligent satire on the situation of mental hospitals and their patients.

- He ridicules life at the 'funny farms': lots of tranquillizers (**54** 5), nosey gits, privacy revealed on couch (**54** 7).
- He makes comic comparisons:
  funny farm (**54** 5)   bighouse (**54** 10).
- He accuses the patients of taking advantage of the Welfare System (**54** 8–9).
- He makes ironic comments on society's understanding for the patients: 'Sickness in the head is as common as the cold. Everybody's at it.' (**54** 3–4); 'Sort of social prerequisite in certain areas. Unless you've copped for the regulation nervous breakdowns, you're not quite 'In' ...' (**54** 10–**55** 1).

Unit 6: The Trial of Paul (**55** 16–**61** 13)

Vic und Terry beschuldigen Paul, wilde Parties im Untergeschoß zu veranstalten und halten regelrecht Gericht. Der physische und psychische Druck von allen Seiten bringt Paul schließlich dazu, sich in einer verzweifelten Befreiungsaktion zu wehren und beide Opponenten als *hooligans* (**61** 5) und besonders Terry als *yobbo* (**56** 10) zu bezeichnen. Beide ziehen daraufhin den Strick um Pauls Hals immer enger. Wieder sollte der Text den Schülern durch Vorlektüre vertraut sein, bevor die Cassette eingesetzt wird.

1. *How does Vic place Paul on trial?*
Vic continues his psychological aggression by moving to and fro: on the one hand he does not keep his distance (*'presses his face close to PAUL's and shouts'*; **56** 4), on the other hand he 'withdraws' by shaking his head (**56** 13), thus indicating his disappointment with Paul's performance. Paul is put on trial and accused of his 'parties', 'orgies' and 'all-night rave-ups' in his 'pornographic basement room' (**56** 4–5). When he – for the first time – loses control (he calls Terry a 'yobbo'; **56** 10), Vic reminds him sarcastically of his (British) education, where discipline is required (**56** 17–21). Paul can only get himself under control by asserting that he is non-violent, (**56** 28), which is ironically questioned by Vic ('Pacifist, are we?'; **56** 29).

Assuming all the roles at court – prosecutor, victim, witness, cross-examiner, judge, 'executioner' – Vic finally drives Paul to desperation by making false allegations against him. Paul is the hopeless object of Vic's accusations and derision. He loses control for the second time ('You're hooligans.'; **61** 5), calls for the police, accuses Vic of breaking the law and tries to free himself. But Vic applies force. He *'grabs his arm and thrusts it up his back.* PAUL yells *with pain.'* (**61** 11–12). There is no help available and therefore no escape possible. Vic and Terry themselves represent law and order. The 'execution' can begin.

2. *How does Terry behave?*
Terry manifests physical aggression. Like a wild watchdog he is always ready to snap and bite ('Let me have him, Vic'; **56** 22; 'Wants this straining round his head.'; **57** 4). He becomes a bit more 'talkative' and takes part in the trial by taking the part of the victim (**57** 27, **58** 13). In contrast to Vic he insults Paul directly ('Prat!'; **56** 24, **60** 25; 'Four-eyed git!'; **57** 1; 'Perverts!'; **59** 26). He forces Paul to use the vulgar expression 'crumpet', while Vic is satisfied with 'birds'.

3. *What roles does Vic play during the 'trial' and how does Paul defend himself?*

The following diagram might help to answer this question:

VIC'S ROLES (LAW AND ORDER)		PAUL'S DEFENCE
PROSECUTOR	– Parties! Orgies! Rave-ups! – Noise! – All night! Till 3!	← Birthday party. ← Friends. ← I'm careful about noise.
VICTIM	– We lost sleep. – We had to stand it. – Terry on the verge of breakdown Terry a bag of shakes; tears! BUT: We didn't murmur/go down/kick the shit out of him. We gritted our under-standing teeth.	← I asked for permission. ← I behaved responsibly.
WITNESS	– We heard giggles! – We live right above you, can't miss.	
CROSS-EXAMINER	– Birds! Crumpet! – Nakedness?! Pornography?! – Perverts?! Homos?! Queers?! – Hobbies? – Bird watcher! Peeping Tom! (deliberate misunderstanding)	← Chicks, girls. ← No! ← Ornithology.
JUDGE	– All fits, don't it? (**61** 4)	← None of your business.
'EXECUTIONER'	– Grabs Paul's arm and thrusts it up his back.	← You are break-ing the law! ← I'll fetch the police!

Homework:

*How does Vic see Terry, the skinhead, and his role in society? (Refer to **59** 27–**60** 13.)*

Vic describes Terry as a person who is to rescue the country from the dangers of too many immigrants. Terry's stint of Paki-bashing (**60** 1) is considered a patriotic and government-backed duty which he duly performs (**60** 12).

The answers to that question might be summed up on the board like this:

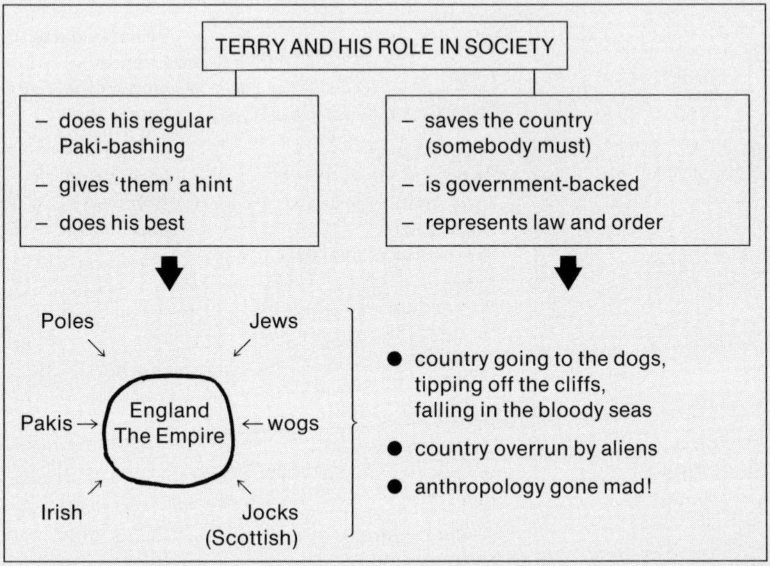

Unit 7: The Verdict and the Punishment (**61** 13–**64** 20)

Dieser Teil stellt den Höhepunkt des Dramas dar. Paul, völlig auf sich selbst gestellt, wird dadurch bestraft, daß er zum *blood brother* Terrys und Vics gemacht wird.

Es wäre eine methodische Alternative, die Schüler zu bitten, den möglichen Schluß des Dramas zu erraten (Arbeitsauftrag), bevor man mit der Lektüre fortfährt und danach die Cassette anhört.

1. *How is Paul morally destroyed?*
Vic treats Paul like a criminal. He warns him to keep still (**61** 18), because he wants to make him 'comfy' (**61** 21) – an ironical remark referring to a similar statement at the beginning of the play (**48** 13–18). In fact, Vic treats him like a person who is mentally insecure, judging from the paternal 'we' he uses ('All we're going to do is sit down again.'; **61** 14). Paul is tied to the upright chair with a rope before Vic announces the verdict: Paul is pronounced guilty because of using words like 'yobbo' and 'hooligan' (**61** 28–29). He is also morally guilty of condemning other people simply because of their appearance (**61** 26–27/30–32). Vic indirectly accuses society of injustice: whereas Paul, the student, is well off (**62** 15–30), 'Mister Breedon' doesn't have a chance (**63** 4–12). Although Paul apologizes,

struggles, begs for mercy, shouts for help, whimpers and protests that he is 'non-violent' (**63** 3), he is finally punished. Vic cuts his hair and Terry, whose chain has always been ready to strike (**61** 17), takes off his 'bovver'-boots and puts them on Paul's feet (**63** 24–25). Significantly enough Vic has mercy on Paul: he doesn't shave his head, although this is suggested by Terry (**63** 22–23). The student Paul has now become a skinhead. He is in fact Vic's and Terry's 'brother'. The climax of this scene – and perhaps of the play as a whole – is Paul's look in the mirror after he has been untied (**64** 8–9). Paul realizes that he is totally alone. Neither society's law and order (= police) nor his role as a student can do anything to help. Vic laughs and Terry sniggers and calls him 'Ponce!' (**64** 10). There is a short silence before the storm. Paul suddenly flies into a violent and uncontrollable rage, thrashes about the room, knocks Vic down and is on the point of hitting Terry with the bicycle chain, when Terry's gesture of self-defence brings him back to himself. He realizes that he has been morally broken. Stunned and incredulous at his own behaviour, he takes off Terry's boots and slowly leaves the room, stammering desperately '... did nothing ... non-violent.' (**64** 17).

Suggestions for the blackboard:

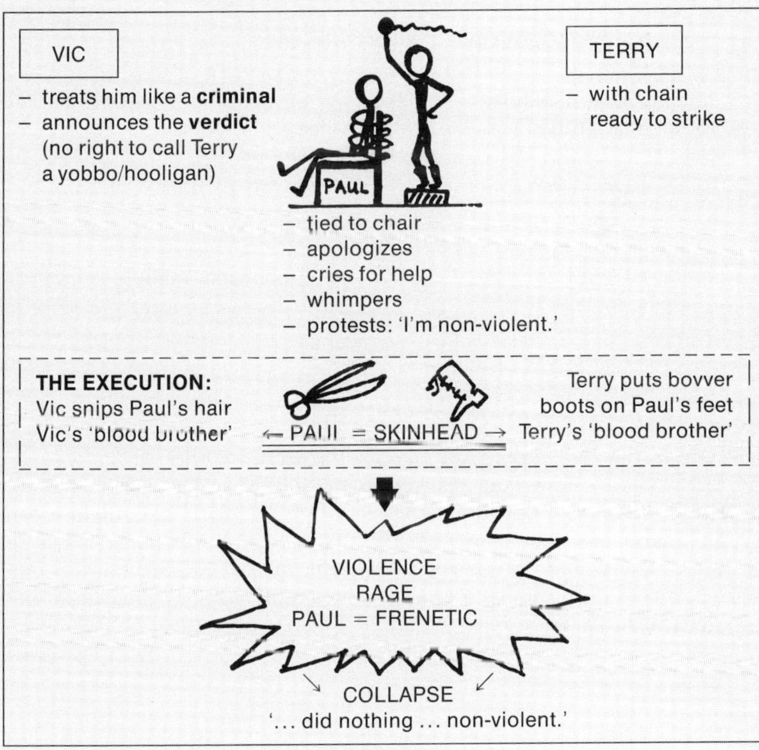

2. *How does Vic compare Terry's situation with Paul's? (Refer to* ***62*** *15–20 and* ***63*** *4–18.)*
Vic points out that both Terry and Paul are very similar to each other as far as their youth and energy are concerned. Whereas Paul, however, is highly privileged, Vic lives in unfavourable social surroundings and is forced to lead a drab and miserable existence. The only chance of getting rid of his 'juices' is 'through bovver' (**63** 14–15). Therefore Vic strongly resents Paul's calling Terry a hooligan or a yobbo. He feels angry about Paul's arrogance, and the way he argues reveals an indirect criticism of the blatant injustice of society.

Suggestions for the blackboard:

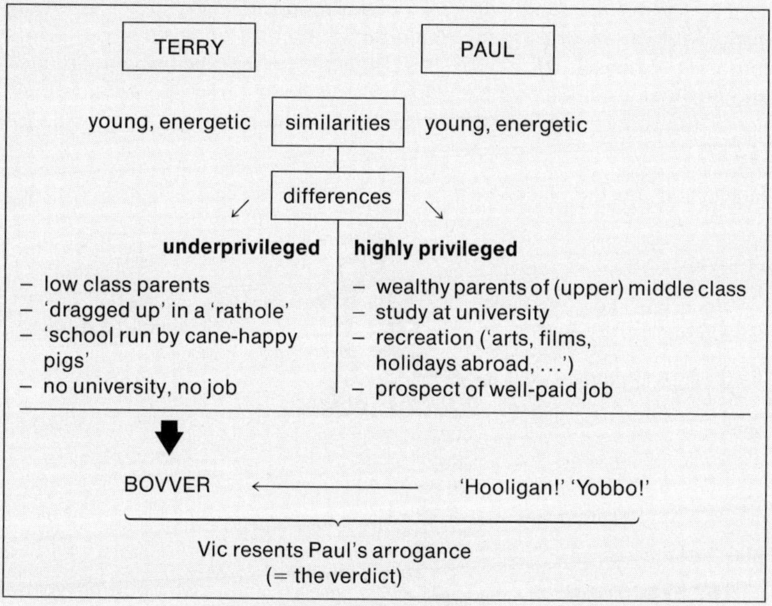

3. *Why does Vic take revenge on Paul for the social injustice he deplores?*
He just wants to show Paul (as well as the audience) that all people are 'brothers' whenever they are deprived of their 'hair', i. e. their roles, wealth, beauty, possibilities and chances. They would probably do the same as Terry: they would try to 'get rid of their juices through bovver' and violence. That's why nobody is entitled to contemptuous arrogance and prejudice. He calls for an understanding of people like Terry.

Unit 8: Further Structural and Thematic Aspects of the Play

The following questions can either be dealt with in class or given as homework.

1. *Retrace the role reversal of Vic/Terry and Paul and try to show it in a diagram.*
The play reveals a remarkable transformation. At the beginning Paul is the decent middle-class student who believes in moral qualities like kindness, honesty, politeness and non-violence. His political credo is certainly based on an unquestioned loyalty to and respect for middle-class values, and the language he speaks is standard and 'polite' English. He plays the role he is expected to play: he is a nice young man.

In the course of the play, however, Paul is helplessly exposed to Vic's provocation. He is unable to cope with Vic's rudeness and can therefore only react. His whole endeavour is concentrated on personal reassurance and the preservation of his identity. At the end he is removed from his safe and rational world. On looking into the mirror he discovers the loss of his identity, turns to violence as a means of solving conflicts. This is just what Vic has provoked, and wants to happen.

Vic and Terry are the direct opposite. Their lower-class background and their 'philosophy' lead them to display violence, aggressiveness, indecency, rudeness and disrespect. One would expect both of them to use substandard English (with slang and taboo expressions). But in fact it is only Terry who restricts himself to that level. Vic, however, who is very intelligent, is fluent in all levels and styles of language. He uses his ability to assume the role of a decent middle class person in order to abuse Paul's middle-class values. In fact, he outwits Paul's politeness and viciously uses this game of hide-and-seek as a means of provocation.

He puts on a mask and enacts a 'play within the play'. At the end he drops his mask and shows naked aggression. He forces Paul to recognize his own real self and experience his primitive urge to use violence under pressure.

Suggested diagram: see p 154.

2. *What might be the meaning of the play? (Discuss.)*
Possible aspects:
- The play is a literary presentation of subculture (skinheads).
- It is a scathing satire of middle-class respectability and arrogance.
- It is a literary rendering of the theme of aggression (deep-rooted, hidden vs naked, outright aggression).
- It shows how people can react to unprovoked aggression.
- It reveals the relativity of 'law and order'.

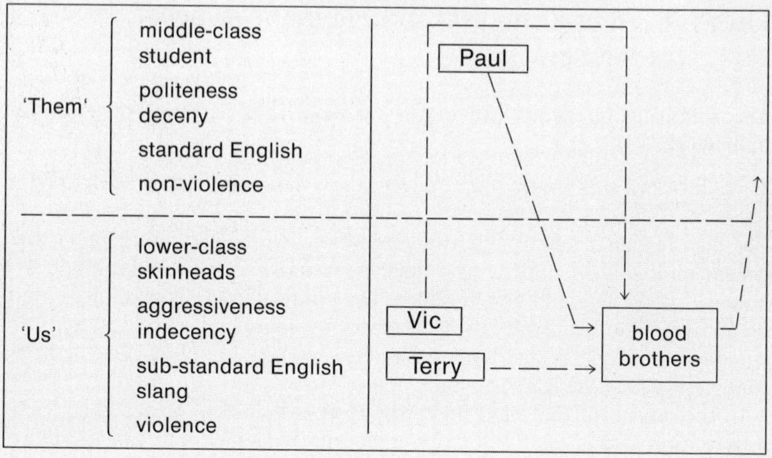

Suggested diagram for question 1 on p 153

3. *'Bovver' has an open end. What might happen to Paul, Vic and Terry afterwards? How might their characters be affected by what has happened? (Discuss.)*

4. *What do you know about the skinheads and in what way are Terry and Vic typical of them?*
The following information about skinheads could be written on the board and discussed:

SKINHEADS
(main characteristics)

'US'	'THEM'
• uniformity	**(variety and individuality)**
half-mast trousers, braces, bovver boots with short jeans (connection with manual work, workmen's clothing, working-class social origins)	– liberals (make love, not war) – long-haired hippies (= Fleas! Stench! Filth! Dirt!) – homosexuals, queers, perverts
cropped hair (tatoos) (association with the cleanness and toughness of the Army)	– 'Flower' people – black or Asian immigrants (they are better off)

- **obsession with territory**

  often connected with the breaking up of the traditional working-class communities (esp. in the East End of London)

  often associated with nationalism (National Front), racism (Ku Klux Klan; Nazis; Hitler; the 'extreme right' in GB; chant: Sieg Heil!)

  they feel a need to protect their areas against intruders (e.g. object to mixed marriages)

- **massive unemployment**

  they hang around, get bored

- **violence**

  open aggressiveness, male toughness, fighting, violence, provocative behaviour, 'punch-ups', 'bovver', Paki-bashing considered as

  – normal
  – a way of asserting oneself
  – stimulating (like a drug)
  – a method of solving social and personal problems

  they are often 'bodyguards' of politicians at political meetings

  they even train dogs to attack people of ethnic minorities

- **language**

  sub-standard slang, 'bad' language, obscenity

– middle-class people

– upper-class people

– students (esp. pseudo-revolutionary intellectuals)

– people who take advantage of the National Welfare System

– rich, wealthy people with lots of leisure time

– drug addicts

– (sometimes even) Catholics

Glossary of Literary Terms

Action: The series of events initiated by the characters in a play. It usually consists of rising action, climax and falling action.

Actor/Actress: The person playing a character on a stage. His/Her performance is guided by the director (or producer) and represents an interpretation of the character.

Allusion: An indirect reference to a person, an event, or a place.

Atmosphere: Mood or feeling created by various factors such as scenery, lighting and sound effects, behaviour, tone of voice and diction of the characters, etc.

Character: A person in a play or other literary work.

Climax/Crisis: The moment at which the action comes to its point of greatest intensity. It marks the turning-point of the action.

Comedy: A literary work – usually a drama – that is humorous in its treatment of theme and character and has a happy ending.

Comic relief: A short comic scene that – for a moment – reduces the tension in play.

Dénouement: The resolution of the conflicts in a play.

Dialogue: The conversation between two or more characters.

Diction: The choice and use of words in speech or writing.

Director/Producer: The person responsible for the performance of a play.

Downstage: The front part of the stage.

Dramatic irony: Words spoken by a character that have for the audience a meaning not intended by the speaker or not understood by the other characters.

Dumbshow: A mimed episode (= acting without speech) introduced into a spoken play (cf the beginning of *Bovver*).

Exposition: That part of the play where background information on the characters and the situation is provided (usually given at the beginning of the play).

Epic theatre: Drama where a narrator relates and comments on what is happening on the stage (cf omniscient commentator).

Falling action: That part of the play which follows the climax and leads to the dénouement.

Flat character: (Cf round character.) Flat characters have only one 'side', i. e. they present one single characteristic trait.

Foil: A character that is used to contrast with another character.

Foreshadowing: Any hints or clues that indicate what will happen later.

Humour: The use of comic elements to amuse the audience/reader.

Inflection: A change in the tone or loudness of the voice while speaking (cf *Bovver*).

Irony: The use of words which are clearly the opposite of what one means, usually either to be amusing or to show annoyance.

Interlude: A short pause in the action used as a theatrical device to make the time between a character's departure and his/her return more plausible (cf *Incident*).

Lighting: Equipment for providing light for the stage and the scenery on it.

Lighting effects: The use of lighting to produce changes in scenery or atmosphere, to focus attention on certain objects or characters, etc.

Monologue: A long speech by one character, heard but not interrupted by the other characters.

Offstage: Behind the stage, out of view of the audience.

Omniscient commentator: He knows everything about the characters on the stage and comments on what they do, how they react and how they feel.

One-act play: A play which – in contrast to a full-length play – concentrates on a single dramatic situation and aims at a single dramatic effect. (Also called *short play*.)

Parable: A story told to illustrate a moral truth (esp. in the Bible).

Plot: The sequence of events in a drama (or story); the structure of the play's action.

Prop: Any article such as counter, chair, telephone, etc. (cf *Incident*) used as part of the scenery on the stage. (Short for *stage property*.)

Protagonist: The main character, the hero.

Reported action: Events not happening on the stage but revealed from what the characters say.

Retrospection: The act of talking about events that took place in the past.

Rising action: That part of the play which brings about the complication. It follows the exposition and leads to the climax of the play.

Round character: (Cf flat character.) Round characters have many 'sides' and usually show a certain development in their character.

Sarcasm: Bitter and ironic remarks intended to hurt somebody's feelings.

Satire: 'Diminishing' a subject by making it ridiculous and evoking toward it attitudes of amusement or contempt. (Cf the satirical view of medical science in *Over the Wall.*)

Scene: A subdivision of a play. (In full-length plays: a subdivision of an act.)

Scenery: The decoration of the stage (including all the props) used to represent the place of the action.

Setting: The place and time of the action.

Sound effects: Sounds created artificially, such as thunder, telephone ringing, radio playing, etc.

Stage direction: Part of the dramatic text that is not spoken by one of the actors but gives information about the setting, the way the characters move or speak, etc.

Stage set: Props and scenery set up and arranged for a particular scene.

Structure: The way a literary work is organized or formed.

Suspense: A state of curiosity, excitement or anxiety which the reader/audience experiences about the outcome of a situation.

Symbol: An image or object that suggests or refers to something else, usually an abstract idea.

Tension: A critical and sometimes dangerous condition in the relationship between characters or in the state of affairs.

Theme: The main subject of a literary work.

Turning-point: The point in a drama at which the main conflict becomes the most intense and where the action 'turns', making the outcome of the conflict clear.

Upstage: The rear part of the stage.